Making Friends with Death

Making Friends with Death

A Buddhist Guide to Encountering Mortality

JUDITH L. LIEF

Shambhala
Boston & London
2001

Shambhala Publications, Inc.
Horticultural Hall
300 Massachusetts Avenue
Boston, Massachusetts 02115
www.shambhala.com

9 8 7 6 5 4 3

Printed in the United States of America

⊗ This edition is printed on acid-free paper that meets the
American National Standards Institute Z39.48 Standard.
Distributed in the United States by Random House, Inc.,
and in Canada by Random House of Canada Ltd

Library of Congress Cataloging-in-Publication Data
Lief, Judith L.
Making friends with death: a Buddhist guide to encountering
mortality / Judith L. Lief.
p. cm.
Includes bibliographical references and index.
ISBN 978-1-57062-332-5 (alk. paper)
1. Death—Religious aspects—Buddhism. 2. Religious
life—Buddhism.
3. Buddhism—Doctrines. I. Title.
BQ4487.L48 2001
294.3'423—dc21
00-047026

BVG 01

To my husband, Chuck,
and to my daughters,
Jessica and Deborah

If all of us would make an all-out effort to contemplate our own death, to deal with our anxieties surrounding the concept of our death, and to help others familiarize themselves with these thoughts, perhaps there could be less destructiveness around us.

—Elizabeth Kübler-Ross,
On Death and Dying

If one knows that what is born will end in death, then there will be love.

—*Sutra of Buddha Teaching the Seven Daughters*

Let us deprive death of its strangeness, let us frequent it, let us get used to it; let us have nothing more often in mind than death. . . . We do not know where death awaits us: so let us wait for it everywhere. To practice death is to practice freedom.

—Montaigne,
The Oxford Book of Death

CONTENTS

A NOTE ON THE EXERCISES

AS YOU READ this book, you will notice that it includes a number of short exercises as well as instruction in meditation and contemplative practices. The primary meditation practice I introduce is a simple mindfulness practice that uses awareness of the breath to settle the mind. It is a simple practice, with a minimum of form. Contemplative practices have more form; they work with the contents of our mental-emotional world. Basically, contemplative practices involve sitting quietly and looking into our experience in some depth. For instance, the contemplation of death is a systematic way of exploring our concepts and feelings about impermanence and mortality. The contemplative practice of "sending and taking" is a way of looking deeply into our self-absorption and our potential to step beyond that.

In deciding which practices to include, I selected those meditative and contemplative practices that I personally have found to be most relevant and helpful in working with dying people and in exploring my own relationship to death. In my classes, I have taught these same practices to nurses, health professionals, hospice volunteers, and others with a depth of experience in working with the dying. I have also taught them to people who were dealing with serious illnesses themselves. They are meant to be put to use. As a rough guideline, set aside twenty to thirty minutes for each of the exercises. Do not rush through them.

In some ways, this is a how-to book—how to get started with these contemplative and meditative practices and how to apply them in your life. If you would like to work with some of these practices further, you can set aside a little time each day to do so. You can take a break from your busy life for a while to work with this material. Then, when you are in the midst of activity again, you can use the six slogans in Part Three as reminders that you can continue working with your state of mind moment to moment, no matter what you are facing.

PREFACE

THIS BOOK is about life and death, and the interplay between the two. It is based on the teachings of the Buddhist tradition — teachings that I first stumbled across in 1971, while living in New York City. At the time, I was a graduate student in sociology at Columbia University and in the odd and enviable position of being stranded in New York being paid to do nothing. I had been involved in the planning stages of a cross-cultural research project, and just at the point when I was to go to India for field-work, war broke out between India and Pakistan. In response to United States support for Pakistan, the Indian government with-held most visas for American researchers, and I was stuck. I couldn't go to India, so I had to stay in New York, and since my preliminary work had already been completed, I had nothing to do.

Eventually, as it was a hot summer in the city and some of my friends were going to Vermont for the weekend, I decided to tag along. That is how I ended up at the Buddhist meditation center Tail of the Tiger attending a seminar entitled "Work, Sex, and Money." The seminar was taught by Chögyam Trungpa Rinpoche, a Buddhist lama who had fled Tibet in 1959, arriving in the United States via India and England. During the following months, Trungpa Rinpoche came to New York several times to teach programs on Buddhist psychology and give meditation in-struction. I didn't know much about Buddhism, but I did know that what I heard made sense and that it directly affected how I went about my daily life. And as I became personally acquainted with Trungpa Rinpoche, I was impressed as well by the gentle and precise way he embodied what he was talking about. The whole experience inspired me to leave New York and move to Boulder, Colorado, in order to study with him further. Had it not been for the India-Pakistan war, I would not have been in

New York, and my life would have taken an entirely different course. And ironically, had it not been for the Chinese communist takeover of Tibet, Trungpa Rinpoche would not have been in New York either. So we met purely by coincidence.

For me, the human factor is important. I went to Colorado because I had a connection with a particular teacher and an interest in hearing what he had to teach. That is what inspired me. Since that time in New York, I have had other coincidental encounters that connected me with people who had something to teach me and who inspired me to make changes in my life. At the same time, I knew I was on my own. Even the Buddha himself told his students that although he could teach them what he knew, what they did with it was up to them.

Once in Colorado, where I stayed for another twelve years, I continued my studies, and beginning in 1975, I was pushed by my teacher into doing a little teaching myself, giving introductory talks and seminars. Although the prospect terrified me, and I would get sick to my stomach even thinking about it, I proceeded with the teaching. Somehow, painful as it was at the time, I also saw that it was a remarkable way to learn. For one thing, I learned that you do not have to wait to get over your fear before undertaking something new. You could just be afraid and go ahead anyway. And I learned that teaching can be the best activity for a student, because the room is filled with people who are all teaching *you*.

I first became acquainted with the teachings of *The Tibetan Book of the Dead* in 1976, when Rinpoche asked me to teach a course on the subject at the Naropa Institute summer program, a few months after my father's death. It turned out that Francesca Fremantle, the translator and scholar scheduled to teach the course, was unable to come. So there was a course without a teacher. I knew nothing about the book and only a little about Buddhist teachings on death and dying, but I agreed to give it a try. About forty students had signed up for the course, expecting a scholar and translator. Instead, they got me, and amazingly most of them stayed. Their inquisitiveness and enthusiasm were such that I scrambled from one lecture to the next, struggling to keep one step ahead of them and come up with something helpful—anything, really—one talk at a time, sixteen talks in all.

It was clear that *The Tibetan Book of the Dead* had tremendous appeal for Western students. At the same time, many people found it difficult to read, as it presumed a substantial background in the Buddhist teachings in general and the tantric Buddhism of Tibet in particular. The colorful imagery and shocking visualizations, the Tibetan and Sanskrit terminology, the many technical references, all acted as barriers to understanding what the text had to offer. But when I began to extract some of the basic teachings of *The Tibetan Book of the Dead* for my students and present them in plain English, even people with no previous background found them relevant and accessible. So I came to see the course as a way of providing relative newcomers access to this text and to the world of Buddhism in general.

As I continued to teach on this topic, I discovered that the people attracted to the course saw it not only as a way to learn something about Buddhism but also as an opportunity to learn about the practice of meditation. They did not just want to develop their intellectual understanding of Buddhist teachings on change and impermanence; they wanted to know how to tame their minds. They were curious to see if meditation practices originating in the Buddhist tradition could be applied more broadly, beyond the confines of a particular religion, and they wanted to see for themselves if meditation practice was beneficial.

Perhaps most of all, the people taking my course saw it as a way to develop a new approach to death and dying. Some of these students dealt with death on a regular basis, as nurses and health professionals or as hospice workers; others were severely ill themselves. So the students took what was being taught extremely personally. Their interest was not just theoretical; they wanted to be able to apply what they learned in the nitty-gritty of their lives and as they went about their work.

I wrote this book at the request of a number of my students, especially students in the course at Naropa University entitled "The Psychology of Birth and Death." Based on what I have learned from my students, I have tried to balance three components in this book: theory, meditation practice, and practical application. By theory, I mean basic Buddhist teachings on change and the nature of the spiritual journey from confusion to wakefulness. The meditation practices I present—mindfulness meditation, the contemplation of death, and the exchanging of self for other—are ways to work with this material personally and directly. Practical application has to do with how to bring theory and practice together in facing your own death and in helping others.

The book is in three parts: Part One is about making a relationship with your own death; Part Two is about using your personal relationship with death as a basis for extending to others; and Part Three introduces six slogans, or guidelines, for developing your understanding and training further through working with dying people.

Without the help of my teacher, Chögyam Trungpa Rinpoche, I would never have undertaken any of this. I am neither a scholar nor a translator, so I am simply trying to take what I have learned and present it as clearly as possible. Although this book is inspired by the Buddhist tradition, it focuses on how insights from that tradition can be applied more generally, by anyone facing the mysterious boundary of life and death.

ACKNOWLEDGMENTS

I WOULD LIKE to thank my husband, Chuck, for his constant criticism, constant encouragement, and constant loving support, and my daughters, Jessica and Deborah, who are always in my heart and keep me (more or less) honest.

I would also like to thank my editor, Emily Hilburn Sell, for her apt critiques and feedback; my colleagues at Vajradhatu Publications, Cheryl Campbell and Ellen Kearney, for their patience; Florence Wald for being a constant inspiration to me; Jacqueline Wurn for giving me a magic potion; my students for their courage and insights; Stephanie Yujas for her careful transcriptions; Alex for carting my manuscript back from Bali; and Jasper for long walks in the woods.

Most of all, I would like to thank my teacher, Chögyam Trungpa Rinpoche, for introducing me to the richness of the Buddhist tradition and its applicability to the very human issues we face.

PART ONE

Ground

Cultivating a Personal Awareness of Death

THE TEACHINGS presented in this book are rooted in the cultivation of an ongoing personal awareness of death. We are on a journey that begins with our birth and ends with our death. At each moment of that journey, we confront the boundary of life and death. We are constantly in transition. At the moment of death, theoretical understanding is of limited use. Many of our ideas are untested and merely reflect our fears and confusion. As we try to avoid pain, we only increase our suffering. We need a different approach. Instead of avoiding the reality of death, we need to look into it and examine our own fixed ideas and preconceptions.

Having done so, we could look freshly at our immediate experience through meditation, or mindfulness practice. Mindfulness practice is a way to drop our preconceptions and reconnect with our immediate moment-to-moment experience of life and death. With that as our ground, we can begin to explore our relationship to death in a systematic way by means of the traditional practice: contemplating the reality of death. Through that powerful combination—mindfulness practice and the contemplation of death—we can change how we relate to death and enhance our appreciation of life. We can begin to make friends with our own death.

1

A One-Shot Deal

LIFE WON'T WAIT. It just keeps moving along, and in a blink, it is gone. It is continually changing. Because of that, we may feel as if we are always playing catch-up. Just as we begin to figure out how to deal with one stage of our life, we are on to the next. We might think, "If only I could go back and do that again"—but we can't.

Our life is a journey that begins with birth and ends with death, and once we begin that journey, we are on our way, non-stop. There are no breathers, no time-outs. It is a one-shot deal. So we should relate to our life now, while we still can—but to do so, we must also learn to relate to our death.

What is this journey all about? No one can tell us. It is up to us to find out for ourselves. If we recognize that we are on a journey, one that we share with all living beings, we can look into that journey and learn from it. But most of the time, we are so caught up with everyday hassles that we lose track of our life. It is too threatening to look at the big picture, so we hole up in our concerns of the moment. We are afraid to look beyond that; instead, we keep busy and avoid the whole issue. Meanwhile, our life is slipping away.

For the most part, we are not aware of actually living a life. Instead, the whole thing goes by in a blur. We lose touch with the preciousness and mystery of the cycle of life and death and our connection with others. It is easy to take life for granted, as though we had all the time in the world. But in cutting ourselves off from the reality of death, we lose any sense of urgency, and life has less value. It does not feel quite real, as though we were in an endless rehearsal for a play that never opens. We cannot quite commit to our life as a journey that has already begun and only happens once.

Our journey is well under way already, and soon it will be over. The starting point is birth and the end is death, and we are in the middle somewhere, between our birth and our death, faced with the question of how to relate to the whole thing. We find ourselves in the midst of life, and fundamentally, we have no clue how we got here or where we are going. That is the context, it is our path, we cannot change it. And how we walk on that path is now up to us. It is entirely up to us.

As children, we may have asked, "Mommy, where did I come from?" If our mommy tried to answer us, we may have learned a little about the birds and the bees and about our parents and grandparents. But fundamentally that question has no answer. Our existence can only be traced back so far. Eventually we hit the mysterious border separating our life from whatever came before; and looking ahead, to the time of our death, we encounter a similar boundary.

Cultivating a personal awareness of death begins by cultivating an appreciation of our life as a whole. With this as our basic view, as we go about our business, whatever we do takes place within the context of that entire journey. So cultivating an awareness of death is at the same time cultivating an awareness of life. We are reconnecting with the experience of *actually living a life*.

How do we work with this journey of life and death? The starting point—the only option, really—is to begin in the middle of things, where we are right now. We can learn to appreciate our journey, knowing that it will not last. Although we have not been here forever and we will not be here forever, right now we have something to work with.

CONTEMPLATING BIRTH, DEATH, AND LIFE

Take a few moments to sit quietly.

Reflect back on your life to the point at which it first began, when you first appeared. When did you appear? Where were you before that? Where did you come from? Contemplate the mystery of birth.

Now go forward in your life to the point at which it ends and you are no longer here. What will happen to you then? Where will you go? How is it possible for your life to end and you no longer to exist? Contemplate the mystery of death.

Reflect on your life now, sandwiched between your birth and your death and utterly unique. Where are you now? What is *this* all about? Contemplate the mystery of life.

2

Riding the Crest of the Wave

WE COULD LOOK at our life as a whole as a journey from our birth to our death, but we should not stop there; we could take a closer look. What is our experience of life right now? What is our experience of our life moment to moment? When we look into our immediate experience, we realize that not only is our life as a whole bounded by birth and death, but each moment within that journey is also bounded by birth and death. So it is not just at the end of our life that we encounter death; we are confronting death at every moment.

Death begins with ourselves. It is a part of our life, a part of who we are. Much as we try to keep them apart, death and life cannot be separated; they are completely interwoven. So the boundary between life and death is present *all* the time, not just when we gasp our last breath. This may not be so hard to grasp intellectually, but experiencing it personally is another matter. It requires that we change our whole approach.

Cultivating an awareness of the immediacy of death is a threat to everything we hold dear. It is a threat to our self-image, to our attempt to make our world solid, to our sense of control, and to our desire to keep death as far from our life as possible.

We have this notion of me and my solid life—here I am, "me," in my secure life—and somewhere on the border of that is this threatening thing called "death." There is this "me" that I know and love—and then there's "death," out to get me. Death is out there somewhere, in the distant future, hopefully—more hopefully still, it is *way* out in the *very* distant future! We think, "At some point—but not now!—I am going to have to relate to this thing, because I know it's out there, and eventually it's going to catch up with me." It is as if our life were a line that grows longer and longer over time. Inch by inch, we fight to extend it, until eventually the Great Scissors comes and—chop!—that's the end of our particular line. We know that no matter how hard we try to extend our life, in the end it is a losing battle. But we are afraid to let down our guard. As a result, we freeze up, like old rusty engines in need of oil.

We maintain that frozen approach to life by distracting ourselves from our immediate experience. When we are not just zoning out, we keep ourselves occupied with thoughts of the past and future. We pile up memories—me when I was a child, me twenty years ago, me and all my little thoughts, me and my experiences of this and that. Then we drag all that along with us. Over time, we keep adding more stuff, more and more and more—and we are afraid to let go of any of it, just like a bag lady with her shopping cart. By holding on to those memories, we try to keep what is already past alive.

When we are not busy thinking about the past, we are speculating about what's going to happen in the future. "I'm going to change my life." "I am going to stop drinking, and then I'm going to help everyone who's addicted." "I am going to get a great job and make a lot of money." "I'm going to drop out of school." By speculating and planning, we try to make future possibilities a reality. In our *heads*, they are real. "I already bought the tickets, so I'm definitely going to go. I marked it in the little box on my calendar, and as soon as I get to that box, I'll be on the plane and out of here." But we do not actually know if any of that will ever happen.

To make ourselves feel more solid and real, we continually

blur the lines between past, present, and future. We try to force all of that into one airtight package. Although it is a struggle to maintain, we prefer this struggle to the tenuousness of the present moment—and for the most part, it hangs together pretty well. But in fact, our life is not one solid thing from beginning to end.

At any given moment, one part of our life is already gone, and the other part has not yet happened. In fact, a great deal of our life is gone for good—everything up to this very point in time. If we are thirty, for example, that means that our first twenty-nine years are dead and gone already. They will not be any more or less dead and gone in the future, at the time of our physical death, than they are already. As for the rest of our life, it has not yet happened, and it may never happen. The boundaries of our life are not so clear-cut. The distinction between life and death is not black-and-white.

We do not actually live in either the past or the future but rather in the present—that undefined territory where past and future meet, on the boundary of what is gone and what is to come. That boundary is vivid but not all that substantial. It is the cutting edge of our life and death. The past is at our back, just an instant behind us, nipping at our heels; and the future is totally questionable. Directly ahead of us, we see our death closing in on us. We are caught between those two throughout our life, from our first breath to our last. It is as if we were riding the crest of a wave in the middle of a vast ocean. What is immediately behind us is constantly disappearing as we ride the edge of the wave; and as we are propelled forward, we can neither turn back nor slow that wave's powerful momentum.

The practice of sitting meditation, or mindfulness, can help us to become more familiar with that undefined territory where past and future touch. The exercise at the end of this chapter, a simple meditation on the breath, is a good way to begin. Through meditation practice, gently, step by step, we learn to make friends with death as it arises in our immediate experience.

We begin to reconnect with the immediacy of life and death here and now. On that cutting edge, death is our constant companion.

Practically speaking, if we want to be more at ease with our own death and better able to help others as well, we need to develop our awareness of this moment-to-moment encounter of life and death. Mindfulness practice is a powerful tool for doing so. Birth and death are close at hand, not just in the distant past and the distant future. They can be seen in the birth and death of each experience as it arises and dissolves. At first, it is difficult to stick with the experience of the immediacy of death; it is a little too close for comfort. But as we become more familiar with this experience, our awareness begins to expand so that our personal experience of the reality of birth and death is ongoing rather than sporadic.

Mindfulness practice starts very simply, with what is closest at hand, the breath. What is our experience of each breath, as it comes and goes? The breath is our simplest, and perhaps most profound, connection with life and death. Our life begins with an inbreath and ends with an outbreath. So our breath has weight; it is fraught with meaning. It is not just dead air. With each breath, we can feel that contrast of life and death, that slight edge of discomfort. When our breath goes out, it just goes; it doesn't come back. Every time that happens, there is a subtle threat, a tiny flicker of doubt. "Wait, I'll hold a little bit of you back, in reserve, just in case. I need you. Don't just go!" And when we breathe in, we think, "Thank heavens! You've come back! I'm still alive!" It couldn't be more basic.

As a by-product of the cultivation of mindfulness, we begin to notice similar boundaries and meeting points throughout our experience. We begin to take note of our thinking, for instance, as a process rather than just a collection of thoughts. Thoughts seem to arise out of nowhere. By the time we notice them, they are already there. We don't know how they got there; they are just there blithering away. But as we settle down and look further, we begin to see that they come and go, too, just like the breath. Thoughts go through a cycle of birth and death, just as we do. Like people, thoughts arise from nowhere, they hang out for a while, and eventually even the most stubborn of them fade away.

In subtle and more obvious ways, the experience of birth and death is continuous. All that we experience arises fresh, appears for a time, and then dissolves. What we are experiencing can be as subtle as the breath or the thinking process or as dramatic as being fired, getting a divorce, or losing our life. That arising and vanishing of experience is our life; it is what we have to work with. As we go about our life, and especially in working with the sick and dying, we should never forget that we, too, are dying.

OBSERVING THE BREATH

Begin by sitting quietly. Take some time to settle.

Once you are settled, pay attention to your breath as it comes and goes.

Start by noticing the inbreath. What is its quality? How does it feel?

Now pay attention to the outbreath. What is its quality? How does it feel?

What happens *between* these two? At the turning point?

Conclude by simply sitting quietly for a few moments.

3
Doorways

OUR LIFE as a whole is a transition. It is not one solid thing. Currently we are in the transition from birth to death. According to Buddhist tradition, after we die, we are also in transition—the transition from death to birth. Over the course of many lifetimes, we cycle from birth to death, from death to birth, from birth to death, and so on. Transitions also take place in smaller cycles throughout our life. In fact, each moment of experience is a transition, bounded by its own birth and death. Within the overall context of our life and the great transition we all face at the time of our physical death, we encounter many smaller transitions on a daily basis. Our life is filled with transitions. It is a continual series of births and deaths.

Transitions are like doorways. When we open a door, we think we know what we will find on the other side, but we can never be sure. We do not know with certainty whether we will find a friend or an enemy, an obstacle or an opportunity. Without actually opening the door and walking through, we have no way of knowing. When we face such a door, we feel uncertain, vulnerable, exposed. Our usual strategies do not hold. We are in no-man's-land. Transitions make us uncomfortable, and they are often accompanied by some degree of pain, but at the same time, they open us to new possibilities.

It does not matter whether the transitions we face are

minute or major dramatic occasions. In either case, they have the power to transform our lives. When one experience has died and the next has not yet arisen, we are not caught, but free. Such moments are precious. During these moments of heightened vulnerability, it is possible for us to see things freshly. This can be liberating, but it can also be terrifying.

Transitions shake up old patterns and provoke us to explore new directions. This was the case for a woman I know who lost everything when she suffered a major stroke. Before her stroke, she had a successful career in business and a loving husband; she was at the peak of her powers. But after the stroke, she suddenly had nothing. Her husband left her, and she lacked the strength to resume her career. She had to start all over, at the most basic level. But there was no way she could put her old life back together again.

At that point, instead of trying to reconstruct her old patterns, she cleared the decks. She stepped back and looked at her life from a completely new perspective. Had it not been for her stroke, she would not have taken such a leap. The stroke opened doors that had been closed for a long time. It awakened her appreciation for life as well as her openness and adventurous nature, which had become dormant. Since she was no longer taking her way of life for granted, she was more vibrant and alive. She was in that rare place where there is nothing to lose and nothing to prove.

Transitions are not easy. For instance, I met a man who had been robust all his life and then unexpectedly began experiencing a series of health problems. It turned out that he had contracted the AIDS virus from a girlfriend who was unaware that she carried it. The man was so distraught at this news that he decided to commit suicide. He tried hanging himself, but the rope broke. So he got a stronger rope, but the window frame where he tied it did not hold. When he made his third attempt, someone discovered him and cut him down just as he was losing consciousness. But at that point, something clicked. He was filled with a dramatically heightened appreciation for his life just as it was, with all its difficulties, and he was determined to find a way to work with it.

Although we are always in transition, it is easier to recognize major transitions in our lives than the more subtle transitions moment to moment. There are so many: our first day at kindergarten, graduating from high school or college, getting married, getting divorced, getting our first job, losing our first job, becoming a parent, and many more. Such transitions stir things up—exhilaration and fear, sadness and doubt, the comfort of the familiar and the possibility of new directions. We can see the way things open up and then close down again over and over as we go through life, and how we take on new identities as we enter each new stage of life. Transitions have a lot to teach us; they are very revealing.

When we hit transitions, there is a unique quality of freshness. It is like traveling to a strange county where we are not familiar with the language, terrain, or customs. At first, everything is vivid and new, almost overwhelmingly so. But eventually, as we adjust, that freshness dissolves, and we no longer see so clearly. We have a new set of blinders, the blinders of familiarity. Once things get familiar, we can again coast on autopilot; we are no longer as awake.

When a relationship is new, it also has this quality of freshness. We take a great interest in every aspect of our lover's life and pay attention to what she thinks, her style of talking, her fears, her hopes, the way she brushes her teeth, everything. But over time, we grow so familiar with that person that we no longer need to pay attention; we already know what we will see. And eventually, all we see is what fits our preconceptions. Since we are not interested in looking further than that, nothing new can enter our view of her. In effect, we have made a mummy out of a living person, and we may not take another fresh look at our lover until we enter our next big transition, such as when that relationship ends. At that point, we may once again really see that person, but in an entirely new light.

Our basic strategy is to avoid the pain of transition. We prefer to define our world, to pin it down so that we can live comfortably within our own definition of things. Even the briefest encounter with uncertainty throws us, and we soon begin to panic. For instance, we may have an appointment to meet somebody at his house. But when we find his house and ring the doorbell, there is no response. At that point, we begin to get nervous. Our mind starts to race: "Did I make a mistake? Is this the right house? The right time? The right day? Did he stand me up? Did he forget?" In the brief time before that door opens, we spin out a million theories. We do so because we are intent on securing our ground. We are uncomfortable with the transition in which we find ourselves.

Securing our ground is so important to us that we may even prefer *bad* news to the uncertainty of not knowing. We are much happier once we can affix a label, *any* label. For instance, when I was in India, I became very sick with a tropical fever. In my semidelirious state, I kept replaying scenes in my mind from an old TV movie, in which colonials were dropping like flies from mysterious undiagnosed fevers while the natives beat their drums ominously in the surrounding forests. I remember the distinct relief I felt when my malady was finally given a label, "typhoid fever," although you could hardly call such a diagnosis good news. In part, having a label for the disease meant that there might also be a remedy. But beyond that, my relief came from the simple fact of there being a *name*, some handle to make what I was feeling less raw and threatening.

We like to "get a handle on things," and we are much less comfortable with experience that we have not yet processed or that we cannot label. But we encounter such experiences all the time, in the transitions from one experience to the next and in the many gaps and discontinuities of life. Such transitions are not just occasional blips; they take place continuously.

How do we relate to these moment-to-moment transitions, the many small births and deaths we experience in everyday life? Do we notice them, or are we simply oblivious to them? Even momentary transitions have a lot to teach us, but first, we need to slow down enough to connect with them. There is no possibility of learning from them if we are caught up in the never-ending project of covering them up. And if we are unable to deal with the transitions going on now, how can we possibly deal with the more extreme transition of our own physical death?

Although big transitions are hard to miss, most of the little transitions in life pass us right by. We jump from one experience to the next, like frogs hopping across lily pads, and never notice how we get from here to there. In that way, we create an illusion of continuity, a pretense of solid ground. For us, there is no pond—only one solid green lily-pad world. However, that is not our only option. It is possible to learn how to be more in tune with the process of life and the fluidity of experience rather than continuing to leap from one secure ground to the next. Working with transitions is a way of opening ourselves to the dimension of change, to experience not yet captured.

To work with transitions and learn from them, we could start by noticing how pervasive they are and how we tend to blank them out of our awareness. We could begin simply, working with very ordinary experiences such as walking though a door, taking a bite of food, drinking a cup of coffee, turning the pages of a book. Stop and notice the process taking place. Note where you blank out completely. For instance, what happens when you eat a meal? At first, the food is on the plate, and then it is all in your stomach. How did that happen? You missed the whole transition. First, there was a cup of coffee, and now it's gone. What happened? Where *were* you? First, we were awake, and then we fell asleep and disappeared, and now here we are again! What happened? First, we were alive, and now we are dead. What happened?

There are many opportunities to work with the experience of change, since every single day is filled with transitions that for the most part go unnoticed. All we need to do is to pause and notice such transitions while they are happening and pay attention to what comes up. When we leave our comfort zone and enter unknown territory, what happens then? Do we experience anxiety, restlessness, or boredom? If so, how do we deal with it? What is it that makes this experience uncomfortable? Notice how difficult it is to stay with it. When we enter unknown territory, rather than immediately trying to pin things down, we could try pausing and letting things *remain* undefined for a moment. Even taking that simple step can begin to loosen our habitual fear of the unknown and undefined.

The more we familiarize ourselves with such undefined moments, the more we can learn to relax with the many gaps in our experience. Instead of covering them over and living in fear, we could make friends with the constant transitions that mark our lives from beginning to end, with no interruption whatsoever. In effect, we are learning to accept death as our constant companion in life.

NOTICING DAILY TRANSITIONS

Choose a twenty-four-hour period in which to pay attention to transitions. Begin as you are about to go to bed and continue through the following evening. Notice the process of falling asleep and the flickering between consciousness and unconsciousness as you approach the transition from being awake one moment to being asleep the next. When you wake up in the morning, before you do anything else, pause for a moment and try to remember what you are doing, and continue where you left off.

Throughout the day, pay attention to the many small transitions you go though. Notice the gaps in your experience, when you seem to blank out. Pay attention to stopping and starting, beginnings and endings, doorways and passages.

Pay attention to your inner world as well, the shifts of thoughts, emotions, and moods, as they come and go.

Try to maintain your awareness through each transition, through each change and transformation. Are you experiencing transitions directly or noticing them after the fact? How does your state of mind change when it is in between experiences? Watch how your awareness comes and goes.

To conclude, spend a few minutes sitting quietly and feeling the movement of your breath as it flows in and out.

4

The Moment of Death

IN THE TIBETAN TRADITION, the journey from life to death is viewed as a gradual transition that continues beyond what many of us would consider the point of death. That view was developed out of the close observation of the process of death by Tibetan teachers over many generations. In the West, we tend to think that our journey ends at the moment of death, that it is all over at that point. We think that as soon as the heart stops and the brain wave is flat, then you are dead. At that point, we get rid of you as quickly as possible: we zip you up in a bag, and off you go. But Tibetans continue to work with people past that point, for they have observed that the transition from life to death takes some time. All through the physical process of death—from the time the senses begin to fail; from the last breath, the last heart-beat, the cessation of circulation; from the time the body loses its warmth and becomes cold; from the stiffness of rigor mortis to its relaxation; and even beyond that, after the body has been buried, burned, or put in the sea—that transition continues. So in the Tibetan tradition, the passage from life into death takes place in stages.

The initial transition from life to death takes place over a number of days—as a rough guideline, three to four days. That means that a person we view as already dead would be seen by Tibetans to be still completing the process of dying. Here as well, many people have noticed that when someone has recently died, they can still sense that person's presence hovering around, as though he or she had not yet left. This sensation may continue for a short time after the person dies, up to a few hours or a few days. Then suddenly the person is gone. We can tell because we feel his or her absence as a kind of negative space. Although you might not know what to make of it, you may have felt this yourself.

Even animals seem to pick up on this. My friend Carol told me a story about the death of her old dog. Carol decided to leave the dog's body where it lay for three days, while she did Buddhist practices for the benefit of her dog. What she noticed is that for the next two days, her other pet, a cat who had been raised from a kitten by the dog, would sniff the dog as she walked by and rub against it and greet it as usual. The cat did not seem to be at all upset. But on the fourth day, as her cat approached the body of the dead dog, her behavior changed dramatically. She arched her back and hissed and would not go anywhere near it from that point on.

At the time of death, we are just at the very beginning of the journey that starts when this life is over and ends when our next life has begun. During the period when one body is finished and another body is not yet in the works, we are without our usual physical support system. The journey is disembodied, a mental-emotional journey very much like the journeys we take in our dreams. The person going through this particular journey is no longer dependent on the physical body and its parts—the heart, brain, feet, eyes, and ears. In this journey, hearing does not depend on having ears, seeing does not depend on having eyes, thinking and feeling do not depend on having functioning physical organs.

Without a body, our consciousness has nothing to ground it, so it speeds up, and when our thoughts are racing, there is nothing to stop them. In contrast, bodies create limits. As crazy as we may be, eventually we get tired and fall asleep. We still need to eat, so we are brought back to earth. But if we no longer have a body, we can spin out of control with nothing to pull us back. Although not having friendly obstacles to bring us back is a disadvantage, there are also advantages to no longer having a body. The obscurations of perception we may have experienced due to sickness and other factors fall away along with the body. At that point, even people who were quite confused can again understand things clearly—even more so than they did before they became sick. This means that it is much more possible to communicate with people who are in the process of dying than we usually imagine. This includes the time leading up to death, the point of death, and the time shortly thereafter.

The moment of death is a profound experience of dissolution. It comes at the point when the elements holding our current existence together have dissolved and gone their separate ways. We have literally come apart. As long as the specific constellation of elements supporting our individual life is harmonious and in balance, our life can be maintained. But once that begins to unravel, our support falls away.

Our state of mind when we die has a powerful effect on our journey through death. It matters whether we start off angry, desperate, or in denial or are able to maintain our awareness and our concern for others. We can see how this works if we pay attention to the transitions and hassles we face now. When we are feeling really great, it is easier to be aware and to think of others—when we are strong and they are weak. But when we are feeling really bad ourselves, it is not so easy. Our awareness shrinks, and we think only of *me*. Others become a distant second—if we think of them at all. To begin to loosen that tendency, when we are in pain, when we are sick, when we are in a difficult transition, when we feel hassled or on the spot, we could make it a practice to cultivate our awareness and think of others. If we begin modestly, with the small difficulties we face, eventually we can extend that practice to include more intense situations.

When death occurs, our old strategies no longer apply, so we are disoriented and frightened. How can we work with this? How can we better prepare ourselves to deal with death? The best preparation is working with our state of mind *now* rather than thinking about exotic things we might do later when we are looking death in the eyes. It is better to learn to relate to death now, when we still have the strength and ability. In that way, when we face difficult circumstances, or at the time of death, we can rely on what we already know. People have different paths and different teachers and different traditions—but whatever our tradition, it is not going to help us very much if we don't actually apply it. The point is: do it now; don't wait.

When all the elements have dissolved, there is a gap, and we experience what Trungpa Rinpoche described as a moment of complete uncertainty. We have a direct encounter with the simultaneously vivid and unreal quality of experience. In a simple, beginner's way, we are given a tiny glimpse of this same experience through the practice of meditation. Because of that small glimpse, we might recognize it when we encounter it. However, if we have not previously acquainted ourselves with that open and vivid energy of our mind through the practice of meditation, we are apt to be overwhelmed by it, and the experience will pass us by. In fact, the abrupt encounter with our own mind at the moment of death is so overwhelming and incomprehensible that most of us go blank. When we hit a wall in the midst of life, it is also like this. When our usual supports suddenly crumble, we are in a state of shock, disoriented, and it is questionable whether our mind will expand with that experience or close down.

Our physical death and the many lesser deaths and losses we experience throughout life—the times when our supposedly solid world suddenly disintegrates—are considered to be especially opportune. Why is that so? Because there is a moment of opening beyond our usual conception of things before we begin to regroup. In other words, what leads to insight is letting go, not building up. We might like to build something called "My insight! Ta-da!" The problem with that is, if it is *our* insight, it is not *real* insight. Real insight belongs to no one.

There are many occasions in which we encounter death, whether it's losing someone we love, losing a relationship, losing a job, losing a train of thought, losing a pen, or losing a spleen. There are many shocks and sudden losses in life. Such "little deaths" take place over and over—and each time, we have a moment of opportunity that arises whenever an old pattern is dropped, a new pattern has not yet formed, and we are left hanging. It happens that physical death is the dropping of a particularly *big* pattern. We are dropping our body itself and our attachment to this very life altogether, so it is more opportune and also more painful.

Each time we encounter death, it brings up the contrast between our attempt to hold things together and the way things keep falling apart. We have created a world that we struggle to hold together—our particular identity, our particular way of going about things, our particular lifestyle that we know and love—and we invest enormous energy and credibility in that. We take ourselves very seriously. Our world matters to us. "Any problem *I* have is a very serious problem. *Your* problems might be due to your state of mind, but *my* problems are *real.*" We really believe we are building something solid and substantial. What happens when we reach the point when all that just doesn't hold together anymore?

When we are in touch with the reality of death, it is hard to take all our realities and problems quite so seriously. The experience of death is too vast for that. Our little frozen world to which we cling so desperately becomes like a tiny dot in the midst of a sky filled with stars. In fact, we are so focused on our tiny dot that for us, there *is* no sky—there's *only* dot. This contrast between dotville and vast mind becomes painfully apparent whenever our solid world is interrupted, when our situation is most terrible and we have hit rock bottom—at the moment of death, when we are seriously ill, when we encounter anything we feel we can barely handle. At such times, there is always the possibility of breaking free from solidity and rigidity and opening into a larger world. We recognize that we have a choice: we can continue to cling to our small world as it crumbles, or we can let that go, expand our perspective, and think bigger.

As people age, we tend to invest more and more energy into smaller and smaller things, so the contrast between pettiness and vastness, dot and sky, heightens. We become anxious and obsess over little details that we were not quite as uptight about when we were younger. As the threat of death comes nearer, people get more frantic and invest their energies in smaller and smaller islands of familiarity. I remember hearing the renowned Tibetan teacher His Holiness Dilgo Khyentse Rinpoche talk about getting older. He was in his late seventies at the time. He said that as you get older, you go to extremes, and fundamentally you have only two choices: extremely vast mind or extremely petty mind. There is less and less room in the middle, so you have to make a choice; you can only go one way or the other. Khyentse Rinpoche's own choice was clear: he continuously radiated that vastness of mind.

The possibility of encountering vast mind is especially vivid at the point of death. However, if we have not learned to see the contrast between our carefully maintained small view and the limitless possibilities beyond that, that vastness is totally threatening. When we encounter it, we do not *recognize* it. The point of meditation practice is to familiarize ourselves with that more unbounded quality of mind so that when we encounter it, we *do* recognize it.

HOLDING AND SELF-CONSCIOUSNESS

Hold your hands in front of your body and tighten your arm and hand muscles as intensely as you can.

Note how your attention is drawn inward.

Now relax both hands.

Note how your attention goes out.

PUTTING HASSLES IN PERSPECTIVE

Begin by sitting quietly for a few minutes to settle the mind.

Note the areas of your life in which you are most threatened or challenged, the themes that currently preoccupy your mind or cause you to worry.

Hold on to one of these themes as tightly as you can. Really look into it and see how it feels.

Now relax your mental hold on that theme and observe what happens.

Conclude by sitting quietly and feeling the movement of your breath as it goes in and out.

5

Strategies of Hope and Fear

OUR SPECULATIONS and theories about death can get in the way of our direct experience of it. It is more comfortable to speculate and theorize about death than to deal with the immediacy of change and uncertainty. If we go through the painful process of unraveling our ideas and theories about death, eventually we will hit bedrock, raw experience. At that point, rather than hiding out in our theories about death or our conjectures as to how we might react later on or our ideas of what we should do when we encounter Aunt Nellie on her deathbed, we come back to what we are experiencing this very moment. We come back to the ground of our own vulnerability.

Usually we do not like feeling vulnerable. We prefer to patch any chinks in our armor as soon as they appear, so that we can project an aura of certainty and professionalism. Like used-car salesmen doctoring cars, we putty over our cracks and flaws, repaint, and try to pass ourselves off as solid. But such solidity is not real. Instead of creating an aura of phony invulnerability, it would be better to relate with our genuine vulnerability and uncertainty.

By examining some common assumptions about death, we can unearth our own personal preconceptions and bring them to light. What do we actually mean by the word *death?* The word itself conjures up a host of vague and troubling thoughts and emotions. At the literal level, we recognize death by such obvious physical signs as the heart stopping, the body not moving, the cessation of breathing, or flat lines on a screen. But that is only a small fraction of what the word *death* evokes. Beyond that very literal understanding of death, we have all sorts of theories of what death is *really* about and all sorts of hopes and fears about it. We need to take a deep look at those hopes and fears and ask ourselves, what exactly is it that we fear, and what exactly are those hopes? The point of such questioning is not to come up with some "correct" view of death. Instead, the point is to examine our own assumptions and beliefs, *whatever* they may be.

Each of us has our own theories about death, and we make all sorts of assumptions about it, but we seldom question those assumptions. Half the time, we don't even know what they are, but we are affected by them nonetheless. Although there are as many unique views as individual persons, they could be broken down into five basic patterns. Each pattern is based on a preconception as to what death is about and the hopes and fears that result from that preconception. These five patterns reflect both our theories about death and our habitual responses to it.

THE GREAT OBLIVION/THE GREAT REST

The first pattern, and a very common one, is to regard death as oblivion, the complete cessation of consciousness. If we hold the materialist perspective that consciousness is impossible without the physical support of a functioning brain, then this view seems obvious. It is a view so taken for granted in our society that we fail even to see it as an assumption. Yet that assumption that death is a state of utter oblivion, blankness, or lack of consciousness is but one of many preconceptions as to what death is all about.

The possibility of passing out and losing consciousness is

terrifying for some people. They see the possibility of the permanent loss of consciousness as a fundamental threat to their entire
identity. But for others, this view of death is hopeful. Oblivion is
not terrifying; it is a release from pain and struggle. People who
are weary and exhausted by life, completely worn down by it,
struggling and in pain, can look forward to finally being able to
rest, in the same way as we look forward to a long, deep sleep
after a hard day's work.

If death is blankness, in this pattern, our response, too, is
blankness. We will go to any lengths to cover death up, hide it
away, avoid thinking about it, erase it from our lives. In modern
Western society, we are curiously disconnected from the reality
of death. We buy packaged meat and seafood that seem only
remotely connected with the life and death of a real cow, lamb,
or fish. We cover our gray, eliminate our wrinkles, suck out our
fat, and compete at being most youthful. We remove our elderly
from view, hiding them in old-age homes and Florida condos;
and we do the same with the sick, the disabled, or anyone at all
threatening. Once they are all safely tucked away, we can then
visit them in controlled environments set apart from the rest of
us. And if someone does happen to die, he is whisked away,
cleaned, stuffed, and made up.

At the same time, death is also an object of fascination in
our society. Bookstores are filled with death books, universities
offer degrees in death studies, and media violence is so pervasive
as to no longer be noticeable. However, that very fascination with
death may only be a more subtle form of numbing out. The
more fascinated we become, the more unreal death seems. We
cover up the rawness of death by glamorizing it as entertainment,
by maintaining the safe distance of professionalism, and by por-
ing through self-help advice. In books and on film, death is more
understandable, more neat and tidy than in real life. The entertainment industry gives us a way to both distance ourselves from
death and glamorize death—without ever actually dealing with

it. We are torn between denial and fascination, but in either case, we are avoiding death's reality.

Even health-care workers who deal with seriously ill people on a daily basis, the very professionals you would expect to be most tuned in to the fact of death, may be uncomfortable with it and find ways to work around it. When a friend of mine was in her last week of life, suffering from terminal cancer, the hospital routine remained inviolable. It kept marching along, like the Energizer bunny, completely oblivious, completely inflexible. The rehabilitation staff kept up her physical therapy, dragging her sad body to arduous daily training sessions; doctors kept giving her medications; nurses kept talking about recovery. This would have continued to the day she died had she not seen the absurdity of it all and insisted on leaving the hospital.

In this first pattern, we avoid death through blinders and routines. Insofar as possible, we just plod doggedly ahead, looking neither to the right nor to the left, and keep the reality of death at arm's length. We work to remove unpleasant experiences from our lives so that we can get on with the business of living—but we are not fully alive; we are numb.

THE GREAT INSULT/THE GREAT ANSWER

The second pattern is to view death as an insult, a mistake, even a punishment. We are angry that we actually have to die. It's not right; we don't deserve it. It doesn't matter if we are good or bad people or even innocent babies—the same thing is going to happen to us all. It is not fair. It just doesn't make sense. We have a strong sense of the injustice of it all. Death is mocking us. It is as though we were the butt of a bad joke. Fundamentally we are irritated that life should be set up this way.

The more we try to understand death, the more we realize how much we do *not* know. We can't get a handle on death; it is totally unknown territory. It is hidden, impenetrable. It cannot be fathomed by our intellect. No matter how smart we may be, we are not smart enough to figure it out. All we can rely on is secondhand reports—and then only if we choose to believe them. People have their views and traditions have their dogmas, but can they be trusted? Whom can we ask directly? The living don't really know what they are talking about, and the dead can't tell us. So there really is no way of knowing. It is galling that death does not subject itself to our scrutiny. We are angry at death and angry at ourselves for being unable to solve the puzzle. We are afraid of the unknown.

In this pattern, our strategy is to try to outsmart death. People have been trying to do so for generations and generations— searching for the fountain of youth, the magical antideath potion. Perhaps we can crack the genetic death code. Maybe we can be freeze-dried and reconstituted. Perhaps we can eliminate all disease and learn to repair all our injuries and regrow all our limbs and organs. Perhaps we can find another planet to populate when we run out of room here. Maybe we can figure out how to live forever and never grow old.

We fight death every step of the way and are willing to resort to extraordinary measures rather than give in to it in any way. Scientific techniques to prolong life can be very potent. Many people have benefited from medical advancements that allow them to live longer, healthier, lives. But as death approaches, it is easy to become entranced with the power of medical technology in and of itself, apart from any real benefit to the patient. In this view, it is an act of heroism to go down fighting and never give up no matter how bad it gets. Doctors with this attitude refuse to admit defeat. In their battle with death, they leave no tube uninserted. They exhaust every possible strategy, no matter how harsh, no matter what the cost, and no matter how much the patient may be suffering. And they make it clear to their patients that to give up is to fail, to "lose the battle."

If we can't outsmart death or battle our way around it, at least we want to be let in on the secret someday. We hold out the hope that when we die, we will finally understand what our life and death are really all about. We expect that death will be our final and most complete teacher, that it will shed light on the unknown and clarify our existence. We long for higher understanding, a way to make sense of our life. We hope that when we die, the pieces of the puzzle will all fall into place and we will finally *know*—that we will unravel the great mystery of life and death. The fact of death reminds us that our view is limited, which drives us crazy—we want *answers*. But at the same time, we hope that in the end, even though we don't understand it now, death will part that veil of confusion to reveal what is true.

THE GREAT LOSS/THE GREAT REWARD

The third pattern is to see death as a force sweeping away all that we have accumulated. We see death as a threat to every single thing we have gathered together throughout our entire life. It marks the loss of all our possessions—not just our physical possessions but also our emotional, intellectual, and spiritual possessions. Our favorite insights, our accomplishments, our experiences, our dramas, our memories, even our body—all our favorite things must go, every last one of them. It is beyond traveling light; it is traveling on empty. We may try to ward off death by accumulating more and more and clinging more and more stubbornly to whatever we have, but in the end, we must give it all away. Rich or poor, we end up the same. To paraphrase a Persian saying, for emperor or slave alike, a shroud takes the same six yards of muslin.

Responding to the subtle threat of death, we pile things up and gather our possessions around us like a fortress. Over time, we become accustomed to more and more. What we once only wished for we can now no longer do without. We rely on all of this as ballast, weight. Without it, we are "lightweight," nothing—and that is what we fear most. Yet no matter how much we gather together, and how rich and full a life we create, ultimately none of that can be sustained, due to the fact of death.

As we lose all that we have in our present world, there is still the possibility of hope. In this pattern, our hope is that we will be rewarded in the world to come. We may not be able to take our earthly rewards with us, but we will receive far greater rewards after we die. If we are successful, we take that as a sign of our worthiness and hope to be compensated in the next world. If we have been unsuccessful, or dirt-poor all our lives, we hope the balance will be restored and in the afterlife, we will be as wealthy as sultans. We hope to enter a world so completely rich and perfect that there is no longer even a trace of poverty. We hope that the streets of heaven will be paved in gold. We would like to get around the painful fact that although we have spent our entire life carefully packing our luggage, we can't take any of it across the border.

THE GREAT DEPARTURE/THE GREAT REUNION

In this pattern, we view death as a departure from those we love. It is the breaking of ties and the loss of all those we hold dear. We would like to hold on to our loved ones forever, but death separates us from everyone: our friends, our enemies, our casual acquaintances, our parents, our children, our pets, everyone. If you think of how difficult it is to lose even one close friend, imagine the feeling of losing everyone at once. When we die, it is as if we were departing on a journey totally on our own, with no means of turning back or ever again seeing the faces of those we have left behind—and we might not even get the chance to wave good-bye. We are utterly alone with no idea of our destination. For many people, that aloneness and severing of ties is what is most painful in thinking about death.

All our relationships, no matter how strong or meaningful or tender, are temporary. There is no way to hold on to them. We will not live forever, nor will our friends. One way or another, we will part. We could pretend otherwise and hang on for dear life, but trying to make relationships more solid by clinging tight doesn't really work. We could avoid getting into relationships in the first place, but isolating ourselves from the powerful force of love and friendship is not a very satisfying answer.

Our fear of separation leads us to try to avoid the inevitability of death by clinging to relationships. We hold on desperately, afraid to let go even for an instant, afraid of being alone. When someone we care about is dying, we throw out our emotional tentacles to try to pull him or her back. If we ourselves are dying, it is difficult for us to let go because we cannot bear to leave our friends behind.

One way we try to get around this is by holding on to the hope that whatever separation we experience will only be temporary. We would like to meet those who have gone before us on the other side, and we would like to guide those who follow us when they, too, cross over. (Of course, our plans only include those of whom we are fond; there are many others with whom we do *not* want to be reunited.) We long for reunion. We hope that although we may be lonely now, when we die, we will rejoin our old friends.

Our hope for reunion may not be so literal; it may be more subtle, perhaps a mystical union with all that is or a merging with some principle, such as universal love or peace. But in any case, what we want is to be united in a way that cannot be separated—unlike all our relationships so far. That is our hope. Our fear, of course, is that we are inherently alone and that every connection we make will be lost.

THE GREAT INTERRUPTION/
THE GREAT COMPLETION

Here we see death as the great interruption. Death sets limits and destroys plans. It is hard to find a convenient time to pencil in death on our calendar, to fit it into our plans so that it doesn't interfere with important business. Death does not necessarily wait for us to finish our projects or our line of thought or even our sentence. If we could put it on our calendar, we could control it; but we are not in control, death is. I know of someone who died in the middle of eating his bowl of soup and another person who died on his way to the grocery store. Death is the threat of unfinished business, the threat of running out of time. It's painful to realize that we can't count on finishing what we have started. We may be writing a book, but we do not know whether we will ever finish. We could be engaged in research, but we do not know whether we will have time to complete it. We have a long list of all the things we'd like to do, but many of those things we will *never* be able to do. My friend Allen Ginsberg called me shortly before his death to let me know what was going on and to say good-bye. In the course of the conversation, he expressed this sense of interruption when he remarked somewhat whimsically, "I guess now I will never have a chance to see Albania."

Year by year, we realize that more and more things we thought we would get around to when we were young are no longer options. At some point, we come up against the limits of life, the limits of time. We can't count on finishing our journey to our satisfaction. We may be on a spiritual path hoping to attain enlightenment or at least *some* realization—but since time is running out, most likely we will die before that happens. We might *never* realize anything really important. We may be just on the verge of making the big time in the arts or in our field of business, and we really could do so—if only we had a little more time. If we work and work with no results, what is the point? In this pattern, we work faster and faster, trying to squeeze in as much as we can, and we are always bargaining for time.

We need to feel effective; we need to feel we are accomplishing something. That is why it is so painful when we can no longer do so. If getting things done is how we define ourselves, not being able to do so is torture. Worse still is having to rely on others to do things for us. Yet that is the case for most of us when we are terminally ill. Until now, we have kept death at bay by constantly staying busy. We think that if we are busy enough, doing important things, there will be no room for death to sneak in. We have evaded death so far by keeping occupied—and now we are afraid to stop.

Our hope is that somehow death will bring *true* completion, that life will come full circle. We want to know that we have done the work we were given to do. We desire the satisfaction of knowing that we have lived our life and completed it in a proper fashion. Here our hope for death is that it will be like the satisfaction at the end of a good book or play, when the whole story is tied together and it all makes sense. We would like to be complete, not incomplete, and leave with a flourish—"The End." [*The curtain falls.*]

Unfortunately, things are seldom that tidy. Usually there is much left unsaid; there are many mysteries buried along with the person who has died. Too late we remember what we wanted to ask and what we wanted to communicate. Often there is no sense of wrapping things up at all; we simply stop midstream. So although we crave the satisfaction of a proper ending, the picture often remains incomplete and sketchy.

WE VIEW DEATH IN MANY WAYS: as oblivion, as punishment, as loss, as separation, and as lack of completion. We have theories about it and strategies for dealing with it. At certain times, we are fearful of death, and at other times, we have great hopes for death. We each have our own very personal and unique perspective on the meaning of death, and we are also highly influenced by our culture and our traditional religious beliefs.

Although we all have preconceptions about death, they are often murky and hidden from our view. We seldom examine or question them. But we should look into them because those preconceptions have real effects. They determine how we relate to death ourselves and how we relate to other people who are dying. When our experience is distorted by speculation, it is difficult to see clearly. We lose the ability to distinguish what we *know* directly from what we have *heard* secondhand, what we *believe* on faith, what we *cook up* out of fear, and what is *wishful thinking*. So it is important to bring our own personal assumptions to light and find out what they are.

By examining our thoughts, feelings, and preconceptions about death, we can learn to distinguish our ideas and beliefs about death from death itself. We can find our common ground with one another, beyond the differences of culture, religion, and theory. That common ground comes from making a genuine connection with death as our ongoing experience.

If we think that we can *only* have ideas and theories about death because we are still far away from the experience ourselves, we are mistaken, for death is close at hand and present in all that we do. Our ongoing encounter with death, that very vulnerability, is what links us to one another. It takes courage to cultivate a continuing awareness of death beyond our theories and preconceptions, but that awareness is the basis for facing our own death and working skillfully with others.

EXAMINING YOUR OWN HOPES AND FEARS

Sit quietly and let your mind settle.

What are your own ideas on what death is all about? What do you really think? You could begin by going through the five patterns one by one and seeing if any of them resonate with your own point of view. Maybe you have a totally different view, one that is not found in any of these five patterns. What is that view? On what is it based?

Now you could look into your hopes and fears. What are your hopes about death? What is it that you most fear? What assumptions underlie those hopes and fears?

Try to dig down through your interpretations and concerns to the underlying experience of vulnerability. When you feel that vulnerability, do your best to *stay with it* awhile, without covering it up, interpreting it, or trying to fix it.

Conclude by sitting quietly for a few moments.

6

Pain and
Suffering

BEING VULNERABLE means being willing to face life's pain. If we try to run away from our pain, we only make it worse in the long run. It is like reaching for a bucket of water to put out a fire but by mistake grabbing the gasoline can instead. The Buddhist tradition distinguishes the pain that is simply a part of life from the suffering that we ourselves create by our response to that. If we understand the distinction, we can learn to accept the pain of life rather than struggling with it. At the same time, we can work to alleviate suffering in ourselves and others.

Much as we might wish it to be otherwise, or pretend it is not so, our life is marked by pain and suffering all the way through. Nonetheless, we keep thinking that with the right strategy, we could live pain-free. We create checklists: If I had a million dollars or good health or better friends or a nice house, maybe then I wouldn't suffer. If I didn't have to live by people I don't like, if I didn't have to please others, only myself, maybe then I would be happy. If technology got rid of all disease and made it possible to live forever, if we were always young and beautiful, then maybe there would no longer be suffering. If there were justice and peace throughout the world, and no one was poor, ignorant, starving, or oppressed, maybe *then*. Yet despite the fact that pretty much everyone would like to be happy and free from suffering, like ol' man river, suffering just keeps rolling along.

According to the Buddhist tradition, there are eight basic forms of suffering. The first four—birth, old age, sickness, and death—are basic to all living beings. Since we are here, we have already been born; and once we have been born, inevitably we must die. Unless we die at a tender age, sickness and old age are sure to come along in due course. These four are facts of life common to all beings, no matter how good or bad their individual circumstances may be.

The second group—not getting what we *do* want, trying to hold on to what we have, and being stuck with situations we do *not* want—are based on the dissonance between our actual experience and how we would like things to be.

The eighth, and final, form of suffering is the persistent uneasiness that underlies all the rest.

SUFFERING THAT IS BASIC TO ALL LIVING BEINGS

Birth

Birth is a time of intense, violent change. It can be a life-and-death struggle, as when a chick must fight its way out of the eggshell or suffocate to death. For human babies, it is a process of being pushed and squeezed through narrow, dark passages and thrust into an unknown and frightening new world. Suddenly we need to adapt to a new way of breathing and learn to take in air rather than water. We go from darkness to light and from being cradled in the womb to being touched and handled by strangers. Unlike when we were still in the womb, we are not continuously nourished through our umbilical cords. Instead, there is the anxiety of needing to attract attention in order to be fed and being helpless to feed ourselves. We are alone and separate and completely dependent on the kindness of others, who may or may not be reliable. We did not just arrive—poof—out of thin air; we have all gone through the process of being born. If we were cesareans, we were just yanked out, and if we were grown in a test tube, nonetheless we still had to leave our tube and enter the world.

In the course of our lives, we experience many forms of birth. We are thrust over and over again into new and unknown worlds to which we have no choice but to adapt. In each case, there is no way of going back; we must go forward or die, so we need to adapt quickly. We kick and scream and resist leaving our comfortable home and all that is familiar to us, afraid of being unable to deal with what lies ahead. Yet at the same time, we have no choice; it is impossible for us to go back.

Old Age

Old age has its own quality of suffering. As we age, our physical capabilities and powers diminish. We are no longer able to do what we could easily accomplish when we were young. We get stiff and brittle and slow to heal. We get wrinkles and white hair, have all sorts of aches and pains, and are no longer beautiful. We may have saved our money and looked forward to the time when we could retire, only to find that it rings hollow. Now that we finally have time to relax and enjoy life, we have no energy left to appreciate it. Our children have no interest in our opinions, and we can't remember half of them anyway. Our youth is gone, never to be recovered, though we may invest a lot trying. We spend most of our time looking back, for ahead of us, things only seem to get worse.

Even though we may not yet be old in terms of our literal physical age, we may already be suffering the pain of aging: the loss of freshness, the jaded attitude that whatever comes up, we've been there, done that. The simple delight of experiencing things for the first time—our first kiss, first love, first job—is gone. Over and over, we find that what we started with inspiration and freshness becomes stiff and arthritic. Day by day, we are more hemmed in, as each move we make narrows our options for the future. So in the course of our life, like a silkworm, we are slowly becoming entangled in the suffocating case we ourselves have woven.

Sickness

Usually, it doesn't take us long after being born to experience the pain of sickness as well. Our life is punctuated by sickness, and with sickness come physical pain and discomfort. We are vulnerable to accidents—to bumps and bruises, falls, bee stings, cuts, car wrecks, assaults, shootings. From minor hassle to major threat, sickness haunts our lives. It is a reminder of our vulnerability and our mortality. Even a tiny hint of our own vulnerability—something as small as a paper cut or a touch of the flu—can be upsetting. As the ethicist Daniel Callahan once said, "Every time we are sick we hear from within what death shall mean to us personally. Illness is a foretaste of death."

Sickness interrupts our day-to-day momentum and disrupts our plans. If we come down with a chronic illness, we are in danger of being cut off from our former friends and from the society of healthy people. We have been handed a membership card in the club of the sickly, a club that nobody wants to join and that most people want nothing to do with. If we suffer a sudden severe illness, such as a stroke, we may have to reinvent our life from the ground up. But no matter what form of sickness we encounter, sooner or later, we make the shocking discovery that we cannot really count on our own body always to be there to support us.

The suffering of sickness occurs whenever we find ourselves in circumstances that are not healthy, that cause us pain, and that we can't seem to find the medicine to cure. Sometimes our circumstances just seem to go sour. It is as though we were infected by a virus from nowhere, and no matter how many IVs we stick in and how much medication we take, we can't seem to make it better. Sickness is fickle: it comes and goes unpredictably and seems to come at us like an attack.

Death

Death is a fact we all face. We can't buy our way out. No matter how often we go to the gym and work out, no matter how pure our living or healthy our diet, we cannot avoid it. It comes to everyone, rich and poor, sane and crazy, good and evil. There is no discrimination, no quotas, no affirmative action. One by one, it strikes us all. We all go through that same narrow gate called death. And much as we may be loved now, when we are a corpse, nobody will want to touch us. Our friends and family will act as quickly as possible to put us away somewhere—bury us, burn us, whatever is most convenient. This very person, this very life, this very body, these very thoughts, these special relationships will all end. Period.

In daily life, we experience death as finality. Often, much as we would like to hold on to a job, a relationship, or even a view, it ends and cannot be resurrected. We do not have the option of going back and starting over. When we miss our chance, it is gone forever. Our life is filled with events that come and go, filled with lost opportunities. What is shocking is the finality of those endings.

THESE FIRST FOUR TYPES OF PAIN—birth, old age, sickness, and death—take place everywhere and at many levels of intensity. They mark the life cycle of individuals, civilizations, and the briefest moment-by-moment experiences. These four "facts of life" cannot be separated from life itself. They come along with life and are an integral part of it. We cannot get rid of them, but depending on how we relate to them, they can either be the terrain in which we live or a source of endless resentment. It's up to us.

SUFFERING CAUSED BY THE DISSONANCE BETWEEN EXPECTATIONS AND REALITY

The next three types of suffering have to do with the gap between how we would like things to be and how they actually are. Because we have such definite views of how things are *supposed* to be, when our experience does not measure up to our expectations, we suffer from resentment and disappointment.

Not Getting What We Do Want

The suffering that results from not getting what we want is very basic and happens all the time. We want to be rich and famous, but we're not. We want to be beautiful and smart, but we're not. We want to be healthy, but we're not. If we are beautiful, we want to be smart; if we are smart, we want to be beautiful. We are never satisfied. Although what we do have gives us little pleasure, what we do *not* have sure gives us a lot of pain. This kind of suffering reminds me of a story I heard the Tibetan teacher Thrangu Rinpoche tell about two brothers. The older brother had ninety-nine cows, and the younger one had just a single cow. The younger brother kept thinking, if only I had one more cow, I could breed it and eventually get a big herd like my brother's. Meanwhile, the older brother kept thinking, if only I had my brother's cow, it would make an even hundred. Neither got what he wanted, and both were unhappy.

Trying to Hold On to What We Have

When we do have something—not exactly what we want, perhaps, but something—we are constantly afraid it will be taken away. This suffering is based on the fear of losing what we already have. Although we might not get what we want, at least we want to hold on to what little we have. But we can't count on that; things keep changing. Just when we figure one computer out, there is a new model. Just when we begin to relax in a relationship, it falls apart. We would really like to be able to take something for granted—anything—but we cannot because change is inevitable. We have to work hard to hold things together.

When we are miserable, we may take comfort in knowing that our misery will not last forever, but that is small comfort, because we know that if we are content and happy, that will not last either. Nonetheless, we try to hold on. We even cling to our own misery. At least it is *our* misery, and as such, it is familiar, oddly comforting. As a child, I was an expert pouter. I could pout for hours on end. When this would happen, my mother would hold me upside down, saying, "An upside-down frown is a smile." I found this so incredibly irritating that I would cling desperately to my pouty expression. Eventually I simply could not take myself seriously, hanging upside down, and I would start to laugh. But there is no room for humor in our fight to hold on.

Being Stuck with What We Do Not Want

The flip side of not getting what we want is always ending up with what we do *not* want. We did not want poison ivy, but we got it. We did not want a senile mother, but we got one. Who asked for it? Nobody.

SUFFERING CAUSED BY PERSISTENT UNEASINESS

No matter how well things may be going, we never truly relax. We are not at ease with ourselves. This uneasiness has nothing to do with whether we feel relatively happy or sad at any given moment. It is that beneath the ever-fluctuating moods we experience from moment to moment, things are never quite right. We are always restless, vaguely threatened. Ironically, we may only notice this level of suffering if we finally *do* get what we want. Sometimes people put in years of effort to achieve a goal— graduating from college, for instance—but once that goal is achieved, there is that hollow feeling of, "So what? What now?" We have been setting one goal after another, but we have no idea what we *really* want or what would truly make us happy. We are suspicious of our own experience. We begin to fear that in the midst of all our success, we are missing the point altogether.

There is a quality of desperation in always looking ahead and trying to secure the conditions of our future happiness. This ill-fated project keeps us occupied, but we suspect that in always thinking about what will make us happy *then*, we are completely missing out on the possibility of happiness *now*. We are com- pelled to struggle with our situation forever, like a never-ending home-improvement project. And because we are caught up in this endless struggle, we can never relax.

Sometimes it seems as if pain just attracts more pain, so much so that it is hard to find the root of it. When we look for the cause, underneath one form of pain is another and another and another. There is no way we can redecorate our world so that there is no pain. We could try drugs, alcohol, or religious ecstasy, but we cannot get around the facts of life. When we try to get around them, instead we just add to them by building a mountain of resistance, complaint, and struggle. This mountain grows so large that it begins to overshadow the original complaint completely. Eventually, we are just reacting to our own reac- tions. It is like a house of mirrors. However, if we connect more directly with the suffering we encounter, we can simplify that whole process. We can begin to dismantle that mountain of self- created pain we have piled up. We may be stuck with our pain, but we are not stuck with our habitual response to it. That is the area we can work on.

Children are more direct in their response to pain. When

young children get sick, there is something very clean about the experience. There are no strings attached: they feel what they feel—aches or fever or whatever symptom it may be—and when it is over, it is over. Contrast that with an adult. Adults can't just be sick one moment and better the next. For us, sickness comes with a cloud of fear and resentment that lingers on. But if we remove all that, we are simply sick, which is much easier to deal with. The trick is to deal with each situation as it arises, without burdening it further with our complaints.

When my younger daughter was four years old, she fell out of a second-story window while playing at a friend's house. She was covered with bruises from head to toe. After she was examined at the doctor's office, I took her home, where she immediately fell asleep. I nervously woke her every half hour, to make sure she had not lapsed into unconsciousness. After a few hours, she woke up and immediately resumed playing as though nothing at all had happened. Fortunately, she was fine. She was simply on to the next thing. I, however, was *not* fine. I lacked the nimbleness of mind to bounce back like that, because I was stuck in my fears about how close a call it had been and my imaginings about what *might* have happened. I was so trapped by my fear that I could not appreciate the reality that my daughter was OK. My pain was prolonged because I could not let that go.

We are all vulnerable to pain. If we do not accept our own vulnerability to pain, we will not accept it in others either. We will avoid relating to people who are in pain or who are not the way we would like them to be. Instead, as soon as something starts going wrong, we start distancing ourselves. The result is that people in pain become very isolated. It's like the song "Nobody Knows You When You're Down and Out."

Instead of running away from the experience of pain, we could examine it more closely. Through the practice of mindfulness, gently, step by step, we could begin to explore this forbidden territory. Instead of trying to keep our mind off it or distracting ourselves, we could begin to unravel the process of feeding pain with our fear. Ironically, by accepting our pain, we could alleviate our suffering. The more clearly we see the nature of our own pain and how we compound that pain by our own reactions, the more skillful we will be in working with other people in pain. So understanding and accepting our own pain can be a real link to others.

7
Meditation Practice

THROUGHOUT OUR LIFE, we encounter the four basic facts of life over and over again. Birth is the experience of being thrust into new situations and forced to cope with them. Illness is the experience of trying to keep our life smooth and predictable but finding that it keeps falling apart and breaking down. Old age is seeing our freshness and enthusiasm for each new experience growing stale, arthritic, and routine. Death is the experience of finality, of continual losses and endings. On top of this, we are repeatedly caught in the disparity between our dream worlds and our reality. Our life is constantly changing, and we are fundamentally unsettled.

With all this change, is there any hope of settling down? Is there any possibility of working with change rather than constantly fighting it, working with our discomfort rather than covering it up? Can we learn to accept our own life as it is? Looking into the nature of change and the interplay of life and death is a start, but theoretical understanding only goes so far. We need a practical method of working with our life, a way of settling in the midst of change, a way of dealing with our pain. The method that I have found most effective, simple, and direct is the practice of sitting meditation.

When I first encountered the practice of meditation, I had no theoretical background at all for what it was about. I had read no books on it, and it had never been a part of my world as a young midwestern American. As a traveler in India, I had seen wandering saddhus and yoga practitioners, but my own interests lay elsewhere, with social and economic development. Although I had been raised in the Christian tradition, I had no particular religious affiliation when in 1971 I was introduced to meditation practice at the Tail of the Tiger (now Karmê Chöling) Buddhist community in Vermont.

The first program I attended at Tail of the Tiger was entitled "Work, Sex, and Money." Those three topics greatly interested me, but not necessarily in that order. On the very first day, a member of the program staff announced that the next day would be an "all-day sitting" outside on the lawn under a tent. Being a generally game sort, I showed up with the other forty or so people and tried to follow along. To my surprise, although it was not at all dramatic—rather boring, in fact—my experience that day changed the course of my life. Amid the shifts and turns, the aches and pains, the speculations about what I should be doing and if the other folks in the tent were more clued in, I felt a deep relief, as though I had finally come home after a very long journey. Along with that sense of relief, at one and the same time, I realized that I was painfully estranged from myself, as though I had lost track of who I was or where I belonged. It was clear to me that there was more to meditation than meets the eye. So I changed course, uprooted myself from New York, and went to Boulder, Colorado, to study with the Tibetan meditation master Chögyam Trungpa Rinpoche—who seemed to know something about it.

The basic meditation I learned has two aspects: mindfulness and awareness. Mindfulness is calming and focusing the mind, and awareness is paying attention. Mindfulness and awareness are complementary. It is difficult to pay attention if our mind is restless. So first we quiet the mind, and then we expand out. Through meditation practice, or the combination of mindfulness and awareness, we learn how to be both grounded and alert. The great Zen Buddhist teacher Suzuki Roshi used the term *readiness mind* to describe that state of relaxed alertness.

Our mind is constantly settling and expanding. For instance, if we look at a beautiful jet-black calligraphy on white paper, first our mind is drawn to the shape of the calligraphy. It focuses on the precision and elegance of the brush stroke and the rich, black ink. As we continue to look, our mind expands beyond the brush stroke to the expanse of white paper surrounding it. Eventually our mind expands even farther—beyond the white paper in its frame to the wall and beyond the wall to the sky. There is no limit to how far it can expand. Over and over, our mind settles down and expands out.

Meditation practice does not have an end point when we can say, "OK, now I'm mindful. I can move on to the next thing." It is the *ongoing* process of bringing our wandering attention back home. Whatever we call it—"mindfulness," "bodyfulness," "soulfulness," or "heartfulness"—meditation has to do with bringing our body, our thoughts and emotions, and our breath into harmony.

Without mindfulness, it is difficult to do anything properly. Without mindfulness, physically we are in one place, but mentally and emotionally we are someplace else entirely. Psychiatrists used to talk about "split personality" as a pathological condition, but we are *all* split personalities, and we all hear voices. It as though we had a permanent committee meeting going on inside us, with one member wanting to go this way and another wanting to go that way, and everyone making comments and suggestions. But this committee never seems to adjourn or break for lunch. It can get pretty annoying, maybe even dangerous. If we are about to crash our car, for instance, we may not have time to call our committee to order to decide what to do. Meditation practice is a way to work with such a distracted and divided mind and gradually tame and focus it. It is a slow, step-by-step process.

Mindfulness is gentle. It is not a battle. Meditation practice is a way of making friends with our mind. We could try to take our unruly mind and whip it into shape, but when we fight our mind, we invariably lose. We could try to stop our thoughts. But the harder we struggle to get rid of our thoughts, the more thoughts there are. It is like the story of the Scythian soldiers in Greek mythology. Each soldier you kill produces many new soldiers. The instant one soldier's blood falls to the ground, more soldiers are born. So the more you kill, the worse off you are. In meditation practice, we let the thinking process wear down on its own instead of fighting thoughts with thoughts.

The nice thing about meditation is that it makes use of what every one of us already has: our breath, our thoughts and emotions, and our body. We have everything we need in order to practice. You may think, "All I have is a foggy and wandering mind, intense and unpredictable emotions and an unreliable and restless body." But those three are all you need. With them, you are very well equipped to practice meditation. In meditation, nothing is left out: we have what we need, and we work with what we have.

The heart of meditation practice is the breath, which flows in and out of us constantly and is the force of life itself. It is to this heart that we return over and over again as we practice. The breath serves as a link between our inner world and the world outside. The physical sensation of breathing reflects our state of mind and body very simply and accurately. Working with the breath is a way of synchronizing our body and mind.

To begin the practice of meditation, we need to take a break from our ceaseless activities. We need to give ourselves a protected setting in which to learn how to practice. The goal of meditation is to develop greater mindfulness and awareness as we go about our daily business. However, it is difficult for most of us to do that if we do not first learn to practice formally, alone or with others, in a quiet setting away from the pressures of daily life. Later, we can extend our meditation practice into all our activities, even the most challenging and demanding.

Meditation is a practice, something you do. The difference between reading about meditation and practicing it is like the difference between reading a menu and eating a meal. It may be mouth-watering to read about all the tasty dishes that are available, but if you are hungry, you need to eat.

Meditation practice is very simple, but it is also very subtle. That is why, in times past, it was handed down carefully from one human to another, directly and face-to-face. Nowadays you can learn the basics of meditation practice from a book, but as you develop your meditation practice, it is good to work with a qualified meditation instructor, if possible.

If you are interested in starting a meditation practice, try to set aside a spot in your house or apartment for regular sitting practice and set aside some time each day for meditation. Meditation, like most endeavors, takes time and effort. Try to practice regularly, if only for a short session each time. Regular practice is like dripping water on a stone. Each drop may seem insignificant, but over time, that water melts through the toughest rock.

BASIC INSTRUCTIONS FOR MEDITATION PRACTICE

If you would like to begin meditation practice, here are the basic instructions, broken down into three parts: body, breath, and mind.

Body

To practice meditation, begin by taking a comfortable upright posture that is not too stiff and not too loose. It does not matter if you use a chair or a cushion. Either is fine. Place your hands on your knees and let your arms hang straight down from your shoulders. If you are in a chair, place your feet on the floor. If you are on a cushion, a simple cross-legged posture is adequate; full lotus is not required.

Go slowly. Take the time to settle into your body, to feel its weight, its boundaries, its various sensations of heat or cold. Let the senses relax; do not try to close them off. If you hear sounds, let them be; if you smell odors, let them be. Do not try to hold on to your sense perceptions, alter them, or get rid of them.

As for your eyes, keep them open and directed downward. Rest your gaze a comfortable distance in front of you. Try not to strain your eyes. Let the gaze diffuse.

Sense the pull of gravity, the weight and solidity of the body, and its simplicity. When you feel restless, settle further. Regard your body as a mountain, broad at the base, connected to the earth, unmoving, weighty, and solid.

Breath

Having settled the body, you can go to the heart of the practice, which is working with the breath. Breathe naturally. Work with the breath as it is. As the breath cycles in and out in a constant flow, begin by noting the outbreath. As you exhale, gently place your attention on the breath going out and dissolving into the space around you. With the inbreath, you can take a little break. You are not neglecting the inbreath, but neither are you particularly focusing on it.

As you practice, over and over you bring your attention back to the outbreath. If you lose track, or your mind wanders, gently bring it back. If you find that you lose track on a regular basis and are always starting over, that is fine. Don't worry about it. Just deal with each breath as it arises.

Mind

The third component of meditation practice is your mind—which, in this context, refers to the ongoing mental activity, both thoughts and emotions, that takes place as you meditate. In meditation practice, the focus is on the *activity* or *process* of mind, as opposed to the particular *contents*. It has more to do with *how* you think than *what* you are thinking about. Some thoughts are more entertaining than others, of course. You may have approved thoughts and taboo thoughts. Instead of analyzing all that, you simply notice that you are thinking and return to the breath, without judging or evaluating the particular thought. You label whatever arises "thinking."

SUBTLETIES OF MEDITATION PRACTICE

Meditation practice is really quite simple. If you would like to develop a regular meditation practice, the preceding basic instructions should enable you to start. As you go on, you will discover that this simple practice continuously deepens as you uncover its many levels of subtlety.

The posture of meditation conveys a sense of dignity and even pride. In this posture, we are strong and upright, and at the same time, we are vulnerable. We have the support of our backbone, yet our vital organs are sheltered by only a thin layer of skin. That is how we are built. We have a soft belly and a strong back. In the posture of meditation, our vulnerability and strength are brought into balance.

As we work with the breath in meditation practice, we begin to see that the breath is not just a mechanical process; it has personality. It reflects the ongoing rhythm of taking in and letting go that marks our life overall. When we are frightened, we gasp for air. When we are nervous or tense, we hold air in, and when we are off the hook, we breathe out a sigh of relief.

Our life begins with an inbreath and ends with an outbreath. The first cry is proof that a baby was able to fill his or her lungs. At death, we struggle to breathe, and each outbreath holds the possibility of being our last. Focusing on the outbreath in meditation highlights the possibility of letting go and our tendency to hold back. We are learning to let each breath go, completely unimpeded. Meditation practice has to do with letting go. It is working directly with the intimate rhythm of birth and death.

Usually we have lots of ideas on what we should or should not be thinking about when we are meditating. We think we should have only beautiful or profound thoughts, nothing trivial or ordinary, and it is embarrassing to find ourselves playing reruns from Nickelodeon or repeating the Pepsi jingle over and over. So we try to encourage good thoughts and discourage annoying ones. We may even feel that the point is not to think at all, so we try to shoot down thoughts as quickly as we spot them. But meditation practice is not based on manipulating our experience to fit some preconceived notion of what should be happening or on picking and choosing our states of mind. On the contrary, mindfulness practice is nonmanipulative. It is about what *is* happening, not what *should be* happening. We are not trying to shape our thoughts, nor are we trying to get rid of them; we simply note them and return to the breath.

When you begin to practice mindfulness meditation, you may be surprised by the enormous amount of activity going on in your own little head. Although it may sound easy to simply sit there, notice your thoughts, and return to the breath—in fact, it is difficult to do. Your mind tends to wander all over the place. It can be very frustrating to find that your mind is so out of control and crowded. You may wonder whether it was always that way or whether the practice of meditation is making it worse.

When such doubts arise, simply label them "thinking" and return your attention to the outbreath. You may find yourself doing this over and over, hundreds and even thousands of times. But that's fine. You are discovering something about how your mind works.

The practice of mindfulness is nonmanipulative. It is based on acceptance rather than rejection. The point of mindfulness is to get out of the way, to leave the mind alone and let it settle itself. You are working with your mind by making friends with it, not by trying to replace it with a bigger and better one. Yet it is hard to give up the notion that there is something wrong, that there is something we need to fix. In meditation practice, our fix-it mind-set gets in the way. We are so earnest, and we try to do such a good job. It is hard to just let things be.

If we practice sitting meditation regularly, over time we slowly uncover who we really are. By practicing meditation, we are inviting our mind to reveal itself completely. This may be difficult because we are used to editing our experience. We like some aspects of ourselves but dislike many other aspects. We are willing to look at some areas but not at other areas. Our usual modus operandi is to try to form an acceptable model of who we are by piecing together selected qualities and ignoring others. Some of us are unable to see our own strong qualities; we only see faults. Others only see strength. They dare not see their own weaknesses and flaws. America being the land of self-improvement, almost all of us would like to take on some self-help project and become "a better human being." The practice of meditation gradually undermines that whole approach of editing our experience to make it more palatable.

Meditation practice is a way of revealing *whatever* is there. It is as clear as a mountain lake. If your mind is racing, it is as if the wind were stirring up waves on the surface of that lake. The movement of the wind muddies the water and destroys its clarity. As your mind relaxes, it is as if the wind were dying down.

Without the wind, the lake slowly settles. Eventually it becomes so clear that you can see right down to the bottom. At that point, you might discover all sorts of hidden treasures. The bottom could be littered with old tires or a rusted auto chassis or even a dead body or two with feet encased in cement. It is also possible that you could glimpse a beautiful fish at the bottom or a geode or maybe even a diamond.

Meditation practice works with who we are and what we have: body, breath, and mind. It is a way of paring down to essentials and reconnecting with ourselves at a very earthy level. Instead of always dwelling in a world of concepts, we can touch a more intuitive core. Through meditation, not only do we become more in touch in with ourselves, but we also learn to communicate more directly with others. It changes our approach to everyday life encounters. Living in the "information age," we tend to reduce communication to the simple transfer of information from here to there, like one person's handing over a bundle of stuff to another. But the practice of mindfulness opens us to ways of communicating beyond words or mere information transfer.

In facing our own death and in working with others, training in mindfulness can provide us with the strength and ability to stick with what we are experiencing, even though it may be difficult. If we invest a little time and effort in formal meditation practice and familiarize ourselves with it now, then when we *do* encounter difficulties, its value will become apparent.

During the birth of my first child, I had a very difficult labor, and because that labor was premature, I was encouraged not to use pain-killing drugs. The technique for dealing with pain taught in the preparatory class was to take your mind off the pain by focusing it elsewhere, such as another part of your body or a focal point in the room. But I did not find that very effective. So I practiced mindfulness, including the pain in my practice. I did not try to take my mind off the pain or get rid of it; instead, I just noted the pain and returned to the breath. By accepting the pain as it was rather than fighting it, I was able to deal with it. Because I was not trying to get rid of it, it was much less threatening.

Mindfulness practice is based on acceptance, not struggle. To the extent that we convey an atmosphere of acceptance, there is greater room for communication and relaxation. My friend Regine, who was terminally ill with cancer, told me that in her experience very rarely were people able to just sit there with her and accept the pain and uncertainty of her situation. Yet that is exactly what she found most healing.

The qualities of being both grounded and aware can be cultivated. It is not simply that you have those qualities or you don't. Meditation practice is a powerful means of bringing about those very qualities. So meditation practice is not just an exercise or a brief interlude to escape our cares—it is designed to bring about fundamental changes in the way we go about our lives. Mindfulness-awareness practice is practical, and it can be applied in daily life, to the most nitty-gritty situations. It is especially valuable in dealing with death and loss and with life's pain.

Mindfulness practice is a practical method of training ourselves to be more fully present in our own life and in working with others. It is a way of taming our mind. The simple nonverbal activity of repeatedly bringing our wandering attention back can help us overcome obstacles such as restlessness, mental distraction, and judgmentalism. The presence of mind cultivated in mindfulness practice can radiate out and have an effect on our immediate environment. The radical acceptance fostered in this practice enables us to include the people around us simply, as they are, without judgment, creating an atmosphere that is healing, grounded, and sane.

8

Contemplating Death

MEDITATION PRACTICE is a way to settle the mind and make friends with the constant flow of change that marks our lives. It is a way of healing our divided and distracted self and becoming more insightful and accepting of who we are. As a complementary practice, the contemplation of death is a way to work directly with the topic of death.

The contemplation of death is a traditional practice in which we look deeply and systematically into the nature of death at many levels and into our *personal* relationship with it. Whether we encounter death over and over in our life or whether we have the good fortune to run into it more rarely, we still need to connect with the reality of death on an intimate, personal level. Even if we run into death frequently or are surrounded by death on all sides on a daily basis, it is still possible not to make a personal connection with it.

A woman who had worked for many years as an intensive-care nurse and loved the job came down with a debilitating illness herself. It was unlikely that she would ever be able to go back to the intensive-care unit, except perhaps as a patient. But despite having been immersed in life-and-death struggles on a daily basis, she had never once taken the time to question what it meant to her personally. When she contracted her illness, she was shocked to discover that although she had spent years helping other people deal with life-threatening illnesses, she had no clue how to relate to her own circumstances. But as she began to practice the contemplation of death, she was able to take the rich insights she had gained through her years of work and apply them personally. She had a way to begin to make her own relationship with death.

Every religion, and maybe every single person, has some concept of death and the existence or nonexistence of an afterlife. There are many different views, supported by religious beliefs, scientific observations, and personal intuition or experiences. If we ask one person, she will tell us one thing; if we ask another, he will tell us something else. Some people seem to be very wise, and they are so certain—maybe we should just take their word for it. Whatever we want to believe is up to us—but no matter the belief system to which we subscribe, we are still left with our day-to-day life and our everyday encounter with death. How in touch with that are we? What do we know about *that*?

If we have taken the time to contemplate the reality of death, it is not so unsettling when we encounter it in our everyday interactions. It is part of daily life, so why not be aware of it, relate to it, and accept it in our world? My friend Molly—whose husband, John, has cancer—told me that some people were drawn to John, fascinated by his illness and morbidly curious. It was as if they were feeding off the experience in some way, like bystanders rubbernecking at the scene of an accident. Other people did the opposite. They avoided seeing John or would try to connect but then switch the focus of the conversation every time the topic became too hot. Because of this, Molly and John were tempted to avoid people altogether because it was easier than dealing with all their friends' trips and discomforts.

Like Molly and John's friends, many of us feel awkward relating to people who are sick or dying. But it is possible to relate to others straightforwardly, regardless of whether they are ill. The practice of contemplating death is a way to break free from the extremes of avoidance and fascination. Instead of seesawing between those two, we can recognize death as our constant companion.

The ongoing contemplation of death, so that it is never out of our awareness, is a powerful form of spiritual training. For that reason, many different religious traditions have practices for contemplating death. The goal of such practices is not to encourage morbid fascination with death or sink people into a dark depression but to stir people from complacency and reawaken their reverence for life. Death is a great teacher and we have much to learn, but first, we must overcome our fears and make a relationship with it.

In contemplating death, it is important that we start with our own, very personal relationship to death. When we are called upon to help other people, we will be more trusted if we are not just passing on advice but can speak from our own experience. But since everyone is different, no two people will have exactly the same experience. So the point of this practice is not to come up with the correct understanding of death but to have the courage to look at how we deal with it personally.

This particular version of the contemplation of death practice is based on traditional Buddhist sources. In this practice, we contemplate different characteristics of death, such as its universality (that it happens to all living beings) and its unpredictability (that you never know when it will strike). By examining the nature of death thoroughly and from many angles, we can uncover our own hopes and fears about it and come to a deeper understanding of the experience of death as it arises in our daily lives. The contemplation of death exposes our feelings about death and brings the subject of death to the surface of our awareness rather than continuing to give it the power of the unspoken and the hidden. As a result, not only will we be more in touch with our own experience, but we will also develop greater sympathy and understanding for others.

A GUIDED CONTEMPLATION OF DEATH

The practice of contemplating death should be done slowly and methodically. Do not rush. During the practice, when your mind wanders, gently bring it back to the topic at hand, much as you would bring your mind back to the breath in mindfulness practice. Keep it simple and personal. All you need to do is go though the text step by step and reflect on what is said.

Begin by sitting quietly for five to ten minutes.

Repeat three times (silently or aloud): "Death is real. It comes without warning. No one escapes it. My body will soon be a corpse."

Read each paragraph and reflect on it.

Pay attention. Do not let your mind wander.

Think of someone who has just died or is about to die. Notice how you feel. Notice the sorrow you feel to lose people you love, the relief you feel to lose someone you dislike or someone who has become a burden, and the indifference you feel to lose people you don't know or care about.

Think of your own death. It is certain that you, too, will die. Imagine that your death is right before you, as close as if a murderer were holding a knife at your throat or you were walking down the corridor to your own execution.

Cultivate mindfulness and pay attention.

Think of the friends you have lost already and those you will lose in the future, for you will lose them all. Think of all the possessions you have acquired so lovingly, for soon you will have none of them. Think of the projects you will never complete, the places you will never see, the answers you will never know.

Think of your body and how it is aging, how it is prey to sickness and stress. Remember that you will lose your body one day, that it will become cold and stiff, a corpse to be buried or burned.

Keep in mind that death comes to everyone. Rich or poor, famous or ordinary, wise or ignorant—every single living being faces death. Think of how hard all beings large and small struggle to live.

Think of the frailty of all forms of life. The slightest mistake can end a life, and a minute change in the environment can make whole species disappear. Think of the many close calls you have had in which only your good luck kept you alive and how your luck could easily turn.

Think of how unpredictable death is. You do not know how long your life will be. You do not know in what manner you will die. And you do not know with whom you will be when you face your death, with friends or complete strangers.

Think of the limited extent of your life and how quickly it will pass. Think of the many beings whose life spans are even shorter than yours, such as your pet dog or cat, or little insects who live less than a day. Think of the many lives lost in the time it takes to do this exercise.

Now imagine that you are in your final decline and your death will occur within days. Think of what it must be like to know it is no longer a dream but reality. It is right in front of you.

Now imagine that your death is not days away, but it is coming this very day, within hours. Sense it approaching you.

Now let it come closer still, to the instant of drawing your last breath. Think of the shortness of that moment.

Now sit quietly and feel each breath as it goes in and out. Feel the life of each breath, how vivid it is and how it dissolves into the space around you. Note the gap as one breath dies and the next has not yet come. Feel the incredible momentum of life, the rhythm of one breath after another, going in and out. Feel the way in which you contact your own death at every moment, with each breath you take. Rest in the immediacy and simplicity of that experience.

To close, repeat three times (silently or aloud): "Having contemplated the reality of death, may I face death fearlessly and help others through this difficult transition. May I participate fully in the ongoing dance of life and death. May I never forget the preciousness of life."

The practice of contemplating death is a challenge to the death-denying neurosis of our culture. It is completely the opposite approach: taking death out of hiding, examining it, and accepting it as a part of life. We may be surprised at how relieved we feel. In workshops, I have introduced the contemplation of death as a guided group practice, followed by unstructured discussion. In these discussion periods, people who came into the class as total strangers have been able to talk about their experiences with death and feelings of loss, sometimes for the first time. We all so routinely bury that side of our life that we begin to feel quite alone in grappling with these issues. It is a relief to realize that we need not hide this aspect of our life from ourselves or others.

Every time I lead such a discussion, I am surprised at how much suffering and loss ordinary people deal with on a regular basis. Usually, as I go about my life or walk down the street, the people I see seem so together. Just looking at them, they appear so normal. They give no clues as to what is going on beneath the surface. Generally, none of us lets on that the reality of death has anything to do with us. In this conspiracy of silence, each person hides his own personal experiences with death. We maintain the pretense that everything is fine. The result is that when we are struggling with loss, we feel that there must be something wrong with us, because the people around us all seem fine. However, as soon as one person drops that pretense, the taboo on revealing our own personal vulnerability to death and loss just melts away. For once, we realize that there is nothing wrong with us. We recognize that even the most cheerful person we meet carries her own secret bundle of sorrow and loss. The problem is that since nobody talks about it, nobody knows.

If you decide to work with the practice of contemplating death, please do so with a light touch. Remember, the point is not to replace the denial of death with an obsession with death but to chart a straightforward middle course. If we can do that, when we face difficult decisions about our life and death and those of our loved ones, we will have a way to see beyond the optimism or pessimism of the moment. Learning to be more straightforward in the face of death results in a greater appreciation of the richness and mystery of life moment to moment. So by contemplating death, we are, at the same time, contemplating what it means to be alive.

Path

Opening the Heart

THE SECOND PART of this book focuses on accepting our own vulnerability as the basis for opening ourselves to life, to death, and to one another. The profound simplicity of death cuts through superfluous concerns and reminds us of what matters most, our personal connection with one another. That connection is the seed of loving-kindness, or friendliness to oneself and others. Loving-kindness starts simply, with the acceptance of ourselves and others as we are. That acceptance blossoms into appreciation and then love.

The meditative practice of "sending and taking" (called *tonglen* in Tibetan), taught in Part Two, takes that seed of acceptance and extends it. We can train ourselves in loving-kindness and compassion through sending-and-taking practice, in the same way that we train our mindfulness and awareness through meditation practice. We can develop greater loving-kindness toward ourselves and others.

We will also consider how we can begin to express that compassion. Acting with compassion is not easy. Good intentions alone are not sufficient. There are many ways in which those good intentions get distorted and our compassion falls flat. So we need to become aware of the pitfalls that arise when we try to put our compassion into action. When we explore our own personal obstacles with honesty, we can bring our intentions and our compassionate actions into harmony.

9

Simplicity

IN A STUCCO ROOM in New Mexico, a group of women are
gathered. They are awaiting the arrival of Sandra Jishu Holmes,
an American Zen Buddhist priest. Jishu had died a sudden and
untimely death from a heart attack at the age of fifty-six, and I
had traveled from New York to New Mexico to pay my respects.
Upon arriving, I was invited by Jishu's husband, Bernie, to join
the women who were preparing to receive Jishu's body.

In the center of the small bedroom is a double bed draped
with handmade quilts, and the small group of women crowd the
narrow spaces surrounding it. From the adjoining room, chant-
ing rises and falls, while in the bedroom, women wait quietly.
On a night table is a bowl of fragrant water and a pile of clean
towels and washcloths. A woman playing a sarod quietly sings in
the corner.

When Jishu is brought in, she is in a plastic bag on a cart.
Gently she is lifted onto the bed and the long zippers are unzip-
ped. Removed from her wrapping, she lies naked and beautifully
feminine on the quilts that she loved. At the head of the bed
stands Bernie, who is gently stroking her forehead, and at the
window whining to be let in is her dog, Muji. The women begin
their task, washing the body, dressing it in robes, and preparing
it for the funeral ceremony to come. The periodic wringing out
of the washcloths adds the music of dripping water.

Jishu's body is cold and stiff but not rigid. As a subtle breeze blows through the room, she appears to be breathing still. I know she is not, but my mind is playing tricks. As I remove the name tag from her toe, I wonder, is this you? Are you still here? The scene of women tending the corpse has a timeless quality, both modern and ancient. Jishu's stepdaughter is present, as is her mother. Some of the other women here are friends, and some are fellow Buddhist practitioners and admirers.

Once the body has been washed, it is clothed in Jishu's Zen teaching robes. Pushing the arms though the sleeves evokes memories of dressing young children to go out and play in the snow. Her mother tenderly brushes her daughter's hair one last time. Mother and daughter touching, a husband by her side, a group of friends, and now Muji by the bed.

It is not easy in such cramped quarters to lift Jishu's body into the coffin, a cardboard box, draped with more quilts. Women clamber about the bed awkwardly, take their positions, and with a single heave-ho, smoothly transfer her to the box. Once she is in place, flowers and herbs are added, and the preparation is complete. Nothing needs to be said. Nothing can be said. It is too simple for words.

After the funeral, when I return to New York, I schedule a massage. As the woman's hands knead my body, I think of the women preparing Jishu's body, and I am struck by the similarity. The simplicity of touch, the simplicity of the body—living or no longer alive—the simplicity and ordinariness of people caring for one another.

WHEN WE ENCOUNTER DEATH, it is profoundly simple, but as we go about our lives, we lose touch with that simplicity. Simplicity is experience pared down to raw essentials, with nothing added on or removed; therefore, it is without deception. When we have lost touch with ourselves and one another, the simplicity of death can bring us back quite powerfully to what really matters.

When we lose touch with that simplicity, we lose our bearings. It is as though we were sailing at sea, busy from morning to night tending the ship. But in the meantime, we have lost contact with land, and we no longer have any idea where we are going and why. Rather than let that fact sink in, we distract ourselves more, trying to take our minds off it. Eventually we are dependent on constant distraction, and we need more and more of it. We feel cut off from the world. The more cut off we are, the more afraid we become. Living like that is not all that satisfying. We long for something less fearful, less shallow, more genuine. We long for simplicity.

We know that we need to pare down if we want to contact anything essential, but how do we do that? It does not work to add simplicity to our many other projects, as just one more thing to do. Simplicity is taking away, not adding on. We can't will ourselves not to be complicated, and we can't manufacture simplicity. "I have been so complicated, but *now* I am going to be simple!" What we *can* do is let all those complications we have manufactured trip themselves up. We can let them wind down on their own. That is what meditation practice is all about.

The irony is that in order to learn how to be simple, we first need to acknowledge how complicated we are. Moment by moment, we are complicating things without letup. We engage in this as an ongoing project, building one grand complicated scheme after another. We have countless ideas about every little thing that we do. Each experience that arises we compare and comment upon instantly, and no perception is left unremarked upon, even for an instant. Not only do we have initial impressions, but we have second-level and third-level and fourth-level and fifth-level interpretations. We size everything up according to whatever our particular scheme of the moment happens to be.

Why do we do this? To avoid pain. The attempt to avoid

pain is the thread running through all this activity. There are so many things we do not want to deal with. To avoid them, we spew forth a continual flow of complications and obfuscations. That is how we lose touch. We end up with this gimmick or that, but we have lost touch with bare-bones experience. The more we lose contact with that simplicity, the more we fear it. Although we long for simplicity, at the same time, it is threatening, for at that level of experience, death is *always* present.

How do we go about cutting through all that complexity? We can't simply snap our fingers and make it disappear. We can't just say, "Begone, confusion!" and get rid of it. It takes more than that. We have to be willing to work with the underlying fear, willing to be in the presence of death. When we are face-to-face with death, the simplicity is so powerful that our fear dissolves. In the presence of death, there is an opportunity to let go of fear. But even when we are not facing death, we can still work with our fear and confusion. Meditation practice is another way to connect with the simplicity of unvarnished experience. In meditation, we contact that simplicity over and over again—and over and over again we see how our fear builds as we lose touch with that experience. Even though we may only catch little glimpses here or there, we are creeping up on our own fear. And step-by-step, we are learning to trust in that simplicity.

Simplicity is what links us with other people. It is the ground of connection. We uncover our simplicity only when we let go of the barriers we create to protect ourselves from pain and separate ourselves from one another. How can we help people who are dying if we do not relate to our own death? How can we deal with crazy people if we do not relate with our own insanity? How can we help people who are afraid if we do not understand our own fears? If we separate ourselves from all that, it is difficult to connect with people with any depth. We come in from afar with our professional advice or our latest theory or our this or that and try to fix things up—but it is as if we were communicating across a great divide. However, if we have a sense of our own death, our own insanity, our own pain, there is no longer any distance between ourselves and others. Instead of coming from afar, we are on common ground. When we trust that simple ground, it is possible to communicate with one another straightforwardly and directly.

10

Acceptance

WHEN THE BUDDHA was a young child, he led a sheltered life, brought up in a wealthy family. His father was a regional king and, as such, officiated at ceremonies and state occasions. One of the annual celebrations was the planting festival, which took place when the farmers were about to sow the year's crops. It was a big event, with booths and games and entertainment, and the local farmers and villagers would come from all around to celebrate. The highlight of the ceremony was the ritual plowing of the first furrow. Only after this official opening of the planting season and the blessing of the crops would local farmers begin to sow their crops.

At one of these planting ceremonies, when the Buddha was just a young boy, he was happily playing with his friends until he saw the plow go into the earth. As the plow cut through the soil and made a furrow, he became upset. The young Buddha was touched by how much life was disrupted and destroyed in the simple act of planting food. He saw the little bugs scurrying away from the plow and worms cut in two. He saw lots of confused little grubs and other beings that used to be down below abruptly thrust to the surface and beings that used to be on the surface buried down below. As their world was flipped upside down, they seemed to be totally disoriented and unhappy. So many beings were suffering.

The Buddha was so struck by this experience that he left the festivities and sat by himself under a tree to think about what he had seen. It appeared to him that just to survive on the earth, inevitably we cause other beings to suffer. No matter how kind we try to be, we cannot avoid it. And seeing the suffering of others, we experience suffering ourselves. We could stop eating meat, we could be vegetarians, we could wear screens over our faces like the Jains in India, but nonetheless we can't go through a day without causing someone harm. Even the seemingly innocent act of growing food inevitably causes some beings to suffer and die. That realization, which took place when the Buddha was just a boy, was like a seed that later ripened and inspired the Buddha to begin his personal search to understand the nature of suffering, why there is so much suffering in the world, and whether anything can be done about it. The awareness of suffering had touched his heart and awakened his kindness.

When we open ourselves to others, we are also opening ourselves to pain. As in this story of the Buddha, when we are aware of the suffering of other beings as well as of our own suffering, kindness arises as a natural response. But we have a tendency to shield ourselves from pain and cover over that awareness. We reject those parts of our own experience that are painful, and we also avoid facing the pain we see all around us. By distancing ourselves from pain, we distance ourselves from one another. We lose the ground of connection that makes kindness possible.

The only way to maintain that connection is to extend our awareness to include all of our experience, not just the parts that we find comfortable. Meditation practice is a good way to begin because it is a process of becoming aware of *whatever* comes up in our mind, both good and bad, painful and pleasurable. We are learning to be open to who we are and whatever we are experiencing. So meditation practice is not just a mental exercise; it is a way of making friends with ourselves at a very basic level.

Step-by-step, we are learning more about ourselves and accepting and integrating those parts of ourselves we had rejected.

As we learn to accept ourselves, we are at the same time learning to accept other people. It may seem that there are always other people around and we have no choice but to accept them, unless we kick everyone out or become a hermit—but just tolerating people is not the same as accepting them. Acceptance is the tender and gentle process of opening our hearts to others, to ourselves, and to our common ground of suffering. Kindness begins at this immediate, personal level of experience.

By cultivating an attitude of acceptance and fundamental friendliness, we can lessen not only our own fear and tension but also that of the people around us. We can actually shift the atmosphere in the direction of relaxation and kindness and in that way be a force for healing. To the extent that we are relaxed and open ourselves, the people around us begin to pick up on it. It is like putting a drop of water on a blotter—one little drop just spreads and spreads.

ACCEPTING EACH OTHER

This exercise can be done with a friend or an acquaintance; it takes two people.

To begin, sit quietly together, either next to each other or facing each other. Relax your gaze. It is not necessary to stare at one another. Take some time to settle your mind, placing your attention lightly on the breath. Do not rush but allow enough time to settle and to be at ease simply sitting together in proximity.

The next step is to consciously include your partner in your practice. As you breathe out, extend your attention out to her, and as you breathe in, consciously include her in your awareness. Be as straightforward here as possible. You are not analyzing your partner's state of mind or trying to figure her out but simply being aware of her presence.

Finally, pay attention to the space between you and your partner and your connection to each other. Into that mutual space, as you breathe out, project a quality of acceptance and simple friendship to your partner. On the inbreath, take in and receive the acceptance and friendship that your partner is extending to you. Feel the energy of acceptance and friendship circulate between the two of you.

To conclude, spend a few minutes simply sitting together quietly.

11

Kindness

WHEN WE SIT QUIETLY with another person, we gradually become more aware of that person's presence. We begin to accept and appreciate him. Those two qualities, awareness and acceptance, are the ground of kindness. But we keep getting absorbed with ourselves and losing our awareness of others. When we are caught up in our own concerns, our appreciation and awareness vanish. They completely disappear!

We might prefer to ignore our tendency to focus on our own concerns and disregard the concerns of others. However, if we want to cultivate kindness, we first need to understand our own selfishness. That is where we begin. We need to stop and take a good look at this fixation with ourselves.

Most of the time, we are so used to being selfish that we hardly notice it. Our self-interest is like a background noise we no longer hear. It is a constant buzzing that we cannot seem to shut off. As we go about our business, we are always saying, "What's in it for me, what's in it for me?" That undertone is there whether we are robbing banks or working in intensive care. Because of it, our actions always have a twist.

With children, selfishness is closer to the surface. If you ask a child to cut two pieces of cake, one for her and one for her sister, her piece is likely to be a little bigger—or if not bigger, it will have the icing flower on it. Clever mothers have one child cut the cake and the other one choose which of the two pieces she wants. In that way, you get surgically exact cake cutting. By the time we are grown-ups, we have been told about sharing, and we know better than to let our selfishness display itself so blatantly. This does not mean it is gone, however, only that we are more sneaky. We may put just one little extra particularly yummy-looking mushroom in our rice—or we might graduate to a more advanced form of selfishness and give away the best mushroom in order to bask in how virtuous we are.

Our fixation on ourselves may not be so crude; it could be as subtle as the unquestioned assumption that we are the center and all else is the fringe. Our attitude is that although other people matter, we happen to matter *just a little bit more*. If you look at a roomful of people, chances are that each one has her little circle around her, of which she is the center and everyone else is the fringe. So everybody is looking out and checking back, looking out and checking back, each from her own little world. It is like a game I used to play with each of my daughters in which I would say, "I'm 'me,' and you're 'you.' " And she would respond, "No, I'm 'me,' and *you're* 'you.' " Of course, this game could go on and on forever, because no one would budge from her position as the center of things.

When we are in the greatest pain, we have the hardest time stretching beyond our own concerns. There is a famous story in which the Buddha encounters a grieving woman, carrying the body of her only child. This woman was completely stricken by grief. She had lost everything—her parents, her husband, all her family, and now she had lost her only son. She would not let her fellow villagers take him or bury him; she refused to even acknowledge that he was dead. When her friends heard that the Buddha would be passing through their area, they suggested that she go and see him and ask him to cure her son. So in desperation, she traveled to the Buddha and asked for his help. The Buddha told the grieving mother that he could indeed help her but only if she brought him a sesame seed from the home of a family that had not experienced death. In great relief, the woman set out to find that seed. But as she went from house to house, she found not a single one that did not have a tale of loss. In her search for the sesame seed, gradually she was drawn out of preoccupation with her own pain as she realized the level of suffering all around her. And when she returned to the Buddha, she was ready to bury her child.

The contemplative practice called *tonglen* in Tibetan, or "sending and taking" in English, works directly with this powerful tendency to focus on ourselves. The practice of tonglen exposes the depth of our self-absorption and begins to undermine it. It is a practice specifically designed to remove that obstacle and the many other obstacles that stand in the way of our natural impulse toward kindness.

The practice of tonglen is sometimes described as a practice of "exchanging self and other." This is because the goal of tonglen is to flip that pattern of self-absorption around completely, to the point at which instead of putting *ourselves* first, we put *others* first. So if I were continuing that game with my daughter, it would go differently: "I'm 'you,' and you're 'me.' " "No, I'm 'you,' and *you're* 'me.' " Tonglen practice goes from the starting point of putting ourselves first, through the middle ground of viewing ourselves and others equally, to the fruition of putting others before ourselves.

If our view is to focus on ourselves, then our actions will tend to feed that view by grabbing on to whatever builds us up and pushing away whatever threatens us. Our habitual activity is to protect ourselves by constantly picking and choosing, accepting and rejecting—but in tonglen practice, once again we reverse our usual approach. Instead of taking in what we desire and rejecting what we do not, we take in what we have rejected and send out what we desire—basically the opposite of "normal."

Tonglen practice completely reverses our usual way of going about things.

Why in heaven's name would anyone want to do tonglen? For one thing, our usual way of going about things is not all that satisfying. In tonglen, as we become more aware of the extent of our self-absorption, we realize how limited a view that is. Also, self-absorbed as we may be, we cannot help but be affected by the degree of pain and suffering in the world and want to do something about it. All around us, we see people not only suffering but, on top of that, creating more suffering for themselves daily. But so are we! In fact, *we* are *those people*—that's the whole point. The confusion we see—that's *our* confusion. All those people we see suffering—that's *our* suffering. We cannot separate ourselves out from others; it is a totally interconnected web.

In tonglen practice, we are cultivating the same tenderness of heart that started the Buddha himself on his journey to awakening. If we are losing heart, tonglen is a way of reconnecting with it. Tonglen has nothing to do with being a goody-goody or covering up our selfishness with a patina of phony niceness. The point is not to berate ourselves or force ourselves to be kinder. If we think we are not kind enough, it may not be that we are less kind than other people but that we are more honest. So tonglen begins with honesty and acceptance and proceeds from there.

In the same way that it is possible to cultivate mindfulness and awareness through meditation practice, we can cultivate kindness through tonglen practice. Through the practice of tonglen, we learn to work straightforwardly with the difficulties we encounter and extend ourselves more wholeheartedly to others. Tonglen is training in how to take on suffering and give out love. It is a natural complement to mindfulness practice, a natural extension of the acceptance and self-knowledge that come as a result of sitting meditation.

TONGLEN PRACTICE

Each time you practice tonglen, begin with basic mindfulness practice. It is important to take some time to let your mind settle. Having done so, you can go on to the practice of tonglen itself, which has four steps.

The first step is very brief. You could think of it as "clearing the decks." Simply allow a little pause, or gap, before you begin. Although this first step is very brief and simple, it is still important. It is like cracking the window to let in a little fresh air.

In the second step, you touch in with the visceral world of feelings and emotions. Each time you inhale, you breathe in heavy, dark, hot, sticky, claustrophobic energy; and each time you exhale, you breathe out light, refreshing, clear, cool energy. With each breath, the practice shifts direction, so there is an ongoing rhythm back and forth. You are taking the habit of grasping and rejecting, and you are reversing it.

The third and fourth steps take that same approach and apply it to specific topics. Start as close to home as possible, with something that actually affects you personally. You should work with a topic that arouses real feelings, something that actually touches you or feels a little raw. It need not be anything monumental; it could be quite ordinary. For instance, maybe someone screamed at you when you were driving to work. You could breathe in the aggression that person threw at you, and you could breathe out to him a wish to free him from the pain of that anger. Or if you are worried about a friend who seems to be spiraling down, you could breathe in your friend's confusion and breathe out to her your strength and support. If you yourself have just come down with a sickness, you could breathe in that sickness and breathe out your feeling of health and well-being. The point is to start with something that has some reality or juice in your life.

Once you are under way, it is good to let the practice develop on its own and see where it takes you. In this case, no matter what comes up in your mind, you breathe in what you do not like and breathe out what you do, or you breathe in what is not so good and breathe out being free of that. For instance, after you breathe in that driver's aggression and breathe out your soothing of that anger, what might come up next is your *own* anger at being so abused first thing in the morning when you had started out in a pretty good mood. You could breathe *that* anger in and breathe out the ability not to take such attacks so personally. In that way, your thoughts follow along naturally, revealing more and more subtle layers of grasping and rejecting.

When you let whatever comes up come up, rather than directing your mind along a particular theme, you find that everything that arises feeds right back into the practice itself. For instance, if you feel bad that you cannot do tonglen properly, you breathe *that* in—in turn, you breathe out your wish to be good at it. Because the habit of grasping and rejecting runs so deep, there never seems to be a shortage of topics for tonglen.

In the fourth step, you expand the practice beyond your own immediate feelings and concerns of the moment. For instance, if you are worried about your friend, you expand that concern to include all the other people now and in the past who have had similar worries. You include *everybody* who has suffered the pain of seeing someone they are close to in danger or trouble. You breathe in all those worries and breathe out to all those countless beings your wish that they be freed from such pain.

In tonglen practice, we start with our own concerns, because those are what usually preoccupy us, but we do not get stuck there; we extend out to others. There is very little in our own experience that has not been experienced by countless other beings. The point is sincerely to include other beings in our practice. By the way, this does not mean only humans; it includes such beings as dogs, insects, birds, even bacteria.

In the third and fourth steps, you are working with mental contents, specific thoughts and ideas that arise in your mind. However, if you find that your tonglen practice is becoming too conceptual or abstract, that it is losing heart, it is good to go right back to the beginning and start fresh.

Sending and taking is coordinated with the breath—breathing in what you would like to reject, breathing out what you would like to keep. You breathe with your whole body—through every pore of your being, you are taking in and sending out. Tonglen practice is based on accommodation and balance. There is continual flow—in and out. For you personally, it may be hard to take things in but easy to give things out—or it could be just the opposite, easy to take things in but hard to give things out. But tonglen is not biased one way or the other; it is perfectly balanced. Through tonglen practice, you discover that you have more room to accommodate what comes up than you might have realized, and you also have more to offer than you might have thought.

There are many ways to practice tonglen. You can work broadly, with whatever arises, or focus on a specific theme or situation. You can work with your own immediate concern, or you can use tonglen as a way of working with others. In any case, the stages of the practice are the same. Tonglen can be practiced when you encounter pain, such as at the dentist's office, the physical therapist's, or during childbirth. If you are in pain, it can be of value to practice tonglen, taking in that pain and sending out the possibility of relief. It places your experience of pain in an entirely different context if you are able to accommodate it instead of always struggling to get out of it.

For instance, a few years ago, I had a series of physical therapy sessions for a frozen shoulder, and I noticed that each time the therapist did a manipulation she ominously called "you're under arrest," in which you lean against the wall and she pushes your arm up behind your back, along with a burst of sharp pain, I would feel a wave of extreme aggression shoot through my body. Although rationally I knew that she was just doing her job, and in fact happened to be very nice, what I actually *felt* was a strong urge to attack and kill her. It was an extreme and visceral response. Then, since I knew that I would be going through this many times in my treatment, I decided to use it as an occasion for tonglen practice. I breathed in my pain, and I breathed out being pain-free; I breathed in my aggression, and I breathed out being free from aggression; I breathed in my desire to kill my therapist, and I breathed out to her my appreciation for what she was doing. This did not make the pain go away, but it did change how I was relating to it. I was able to relax and incorporate the pain of the treatment. It no longer filled my entire perceptual field, but it had space around it. I even found some humor in my situation and my state of mind.

If you are sick, that is also a good time to practice tonglen, taking in that sickness and sending out your wish for recovery. I had a friend who was sick for a very long time with recurrent breast cancer, which eventually spread throughout her body. As she struggled with her disease, she began to visualize that on the inbreath, she was taking in healthy energy that was clean and clear, and on the outbreath, she was breathing out her cancer, which was ugly and murky. She was trying to get rid of her cancer and replace it with health. When she talked to Trungpa Rinpoche about this practice, he was very concerned and told her that she was doing exactly the opposite of what she should be doing. She was making things worse for herself by not accepting her cancer and working with it on that basis, and making things worse for others by projecting her negativity out toward them. He told her to practice tonglen instead. The odd thing is that once she changed her practice, her condition stabilized and she lived far longer than anyone had expected. During this period of borrowed time, she was able to make a real breakthrough in her understanding of life and her relationship to death.

Tonglen practice can be done for someone who is sick, dying, or in trouble. In that case, on the inbreath, you take in that person's suffering or trouble, and on the outbreath, you project out to him your health and strength. It can be done to help ease a person's fear of dying, breathing in his fear and breathing out to him your courage and companionship. You could do tonglen for anyone, not just for the special people you care most about but also for those who are not so close and even for people you dislike.

Many people have told me that tonglen is the most useful practice they know for working with the dying. Just sitting in a room with someone, practicing tonglen, provides the dying person with an unbiased kind of support that is loving but at the same time willing to let go. Even busy health professionals have told me that simply taking the attitude of tonglen changes the way they go about their work. Dealing with suffering on a daily basis can take a heavy toll on health workers. Although it is painful to care too deeply about the people we work with, it is also painful to close off our feelings and just push through. Tonglen gives people a way to work with the suffering they encounter and their personal response to it and to include that experience rather than reject it.

Tonglen practice is a radical departure from our usual way of going about things. It may seem threatening, and even crazy, but it strikes at a very core point—how we barricade ourselves from pain and lose our connection with one another. The irony is that the barricades we create do not help all that much; they just make things worse. We end up more fearful, less willing to extend ourselves, and stunted in our ability to express any true kindness. Tonglen pokes holes in those self-created barricades.

Tonglen is always about connection: making a genuine connection with ourselves and others. It is a practice that draws us out beyond our own concerns to an appreciation that no matter what we happen to be going through, others, too, have gone through experiences just as intense. In tonglen, we are continually expanding our perspective beyond our small, self-preoccupied world. The less we restrict our world, the more of it we can take in—and at the same time, we find that we also have much more to give.

12

Compassion

COMPASSION IS INHERENT in our very nature as human beings. It is natural to us. We do not need to create it. Cultivating
compassion does not mean injecting some new, improved element into ourselves so that we can work more effectively. Instead, we simply uncover the compassion that is already there.
How do we begin? We begin by examining the ways in which
we mask this fundamental human quality.

Compassion has three major components: awareness,
friendliness, and openness. We begin with awareness because it
is important at the start to be clear about who we are—not who
we wish to be, not who we hope we are, and not what others
have told us we are or should be. When we are not constantly
struggling to *be* something or somebody, we are not so hampered
by our preconceptions, and we can see more clearly.

Friendliness is an extension of awareness because, as we become more honest with ourselves, more willing to drop false
identities, we feel a fresh sense of appreciation for who we are. It
is a relief when we have nothing left to hide and nothing in
particular to promote. The warmth and appreciation that we feel
when we begin to accept ourselves leads, in turn, to an increased
appreciation of others.

By cultivating both awareness and friendliness, we also
begin to develop greater openness. As a result of greater

awareness, experiences and identities that we took to be solid begin to crumble. We are less caught in fixed views and more open to new perspectives. As a result of greater friendliness, we begin to be more appreciative of ourselves and others. Not only are our views less solid, but our heart also begins to open up. By cultivating awareness, friendliness, and openness, we are making room for compassion to peek through. We discover that if there is an opening for it, compassion is *always* present. Compassion arises on its own if we let it. It does not need to be forced but arises as a natural and appropriate response to the need at hand.

Compassion is based on empathy, being touched by the suffering of others. There are many levels of empathy. Someone who is greatly compassionate is so touched by the suffering of others that it cuts him deeply. He feels its sharpness as if it were a hair brushing the surface of his eye. Most of us are not that sensitive. When we notice the suffering of others, it is more like a hair brushing the palm of our hand. Often, our sensitivity to suffering is limited. On top of that, we have learned to harden our hearts further as a way of coping with the intensity of life and death. But it is possible to reverse this closing-down process and reconnect with our own heart. Instead of hiding from suffering, we could let ourselves feel its sharpness. Then our awareness, friendliness, and openness can blossom into true compassion, which is the will and commitment to help all beings and to relieve suffering whenever we encounter it.

Compassion is easy to talk about but not so easy to apply. Simply reading about awareness does not make us aware, any more than just reading about kindness makes us kind. We need more than theoretical understanding—we need training. Meditation and tonglen are a good start because they enable us to work directly and personally with two major obstacles to compassionate activity: distractedness and self-absorption. When we try to put compassion into action, we come up against those two obstacles continually.

In meditation practice, we begin to notice many things about ourselves: how difficult it is simply to be present without distraction; how often our mind is one place and our body somewhere else; how we cling to certain thoughts or feelings and avoid others. So meditation practice provides us with a method of discovering who we are and how we operate. In tonglen, we come face-to-face with the entrenched power of our own self-centeredness and how difficult it is to reverse that. Tonglen exposes our pretensions and heavy-handedness and points us instead in the direction of humor and friendliness.

Meditation and tonglen provide a strong foundation for compassion, but it is in actually trying to apply compassion in our daily lives that we learn the most. That is when we see the many gaps between our theoretical understanding and how we actually go about things. Each time we lose sight of awareness, friendliness, and openness, we run into problems, for we are no longer expressing real compassion but compassion with a twist. When that happens, our misguided display of so-called compassion really does no one any good. Not only is it unhelpful; it can even make matters worse.

Putting Compassion into Action: Obstacles and Pitfalls

When we try to put our compassion into action, often we are not all that successful, despite our good intentions. We run into all sorts of obstacles and pitfalls, which we will now discuss. We can learn from those pitfalls. They teach us how to distinguish true compassion from a more distorted, self-serving variety.

Prepackaged Compassion

In order to mask our own fear and unease, we may employ prepackaged compassion—arming ourselves with simplistic advice and ready-made strategies, and relying on formulas rather than awareness. It is like donning armor before going into battle. I once saw a video of a person working with a dying man with AIDS in which this armored strategy was in evidence. The patient was lying in his bed, very weak and unable to communicate without real difficulty. When his helper entered the room—with no introduction and giving the sick man no chance to respond—he came right over, sat down on the bed, and immediately began lecturing the sick man as to what he should be experiencing. Then he proceeded to read to him from *The Tibetan Book of the Dead.* As a genuinely kindhearted person committed to spending time with that man and others like him, he clearly was trying to help. But I had the impression that he was in such a rush to present his version of help that he ended up distancing himself from what was going on instead. He came in armed with advice and ready to apply it willy-nilly to whoever was in that bed. And of course, there was no way the sick man could avoid him or get away. Maybe what he did was helpful, maybe not. The point is, he did not stop to listen or try to see what was going on; he just walked right in. The whole interaction was a one-way street.

When we are uncomfortable, we look for ready-made strategies to prop us up. But that approach cuts us off from the people we are trying to help. However, when we are in touch with our own discomfort, we are not as threatened by the pain we see in others, and we can take a moment to connect before applying a particular strategy. We can appreciate that mutual vulnerability as a meeting point rather than something to avoid.

Manipulative Compassion

Another trap is manipulative compassion, in which we are so determined to help that we will even go so far as to ignore the objections of the people we purport to be helping. In fact, once our compassion kicks in, we hardly even acknowledge another's existence at all. We are like compassion bulldozers, more invested in the *project* of helping than in the *people* "being helped." Basically, we look down on people as they are and try to help them by making them more like ourselves. We want them to handle things the way we would and to do things the right way—our way—because we know what's best for them. It is a very uneven playing field. Our view reigns supreme. "Those people" should want our help—and appreciate it once they get it.

An example of manipulative compassion is the deathbed conversion. Having decided that our own religion is just what the dying person needs, we take advantage of that person's weakened state to pressure him into signing on the dotted line while there is still time. We may not go so far as to demand an outright conversion. We just blithely ignore the dying person's own tradition or nontradition and impose on him the religious forms and values that make sense to us.

If we are on the receiving end of this type of compassion, accepting help is an admission of failure, weakness, or inferiority. Being a target of such compassion feels more like being attacked than being helped. If we do not go along with it, such compassion quickly turns to anger. When we dig in our heels and refuse to be manipulated, our helper dismisses us in a huff: "What's your problem? I was only trying to help!"

Manipulative compassion has lots of strings attached: we are offended if our offer of help is rejected; we are offended if our help, once given, is not fully appreciated; we are upset if the people we help do not show results. We expect a considerable return on our little investment of compassion.

The Compassion Credential

Then there is compassion, the credential. We gain this credential by making use of other people's misfortunes to bolster our own personal identity. We are attached to the idea of being a compassionate person, and we thrive on helping people. That is what we are *known* for, after all. In this case, our own image is what really matters most. We want to be seen as knights in shining armor saving damsels in distress. Each person we save adds to our reputation. Because we need to cure people, those who cannot be cured or saved are a threat to our ambition. This contributes to the keep-'em-alive-at-all-costs-no-matter-what-the-consequences syndrome so common in our medical system.

In manipulative compassion, our focus was outward, on results. When we tried to help someone, our concern was to ensure that the effort actually had an effect on that person that could be recognized and appreciated. When we seek the compassion credential, on the other hand, the focus is inward. What matters to us is that our compassion be noticed—that *we* be noticed. Whether our attempt to help works or not, we want people see how hard we are trying, how much we care.

When we rely on compassion as a credential or an identity, we may want to be knights, but we are more apt to become vampires. We reach the point where we *need* people to save. Basically, we are feeding off people, and each person we save nourishes us further. As we feed off unfortunate people, we suck them dry as we ourselves bloat up. As we become more and more pious about all the sacrifices we have made for their benefit, they become weaker, more guilty, and increasingly dependent on us.

We *need* the people around us to be weak so that we can display our compassion for all to see. We need people to be dependent on us. It is like parents who are threatened when their children begin to show signs of independence. Such people need their children to be dependent. Because of that, they become overprotective and try to shield their children from the hazards of growing up. But in the guise of protecting their children, such parents are really protecting themselves. They are afraid of losing their identity as concerned parents, their compassion credential. When we are attached to being caregivers, if we have no one to care for, we lose the whole basis of our identity.

Rush-Job Compassion

One way to help without really connecting is to go faster and faster—to engage in rush-job compassion. If we are distressed by what we encounter, and we don't really want to relate to it, we get increasingly speedy. We just want to do something quick and get out. We are afraid to slow down, because then we might feel something. We might be touched by another person.

My husband leads the Greyston Foundation, which works with formerly homeless people in Yonkers, New York. He has learned a lot about compassion from the people he works with, for people who have lived on the street of necessity become astute observers of the way various people express their charity. With rush-job compassion, it is possible for us to give money to a panhandler without making any connection whatsoever. We can express our compassion without even *seeing* him. Even in the act of giving someone a handout, we can maintain a protective barrier separating us from him.

By maintaining such a barrier, we can keep that person at a distance. We can make him less threatening. We can wall ourselves off from his pain. People who have begged on the streets can testify to the pain of being on the receiving end of rush-job compassion. They get their handout, but there is no human contact. They are literally invisible. The very people who seem to be helping them are in fact completely dismissing them.

If we are always in a hurry, we miss important clues as to what is going on and what is needed. It takes time to look around and see what is happening. It takes time to tune in to the person we are helping and the environment around her. It takes time to settle our mind. By rushing, we limit our awareness, stifle our feelings, and close off the possibility of openness.

Guilt-Based Compassion

With guilt-based compassion, we buy into some theory as to what we are supposed to feel around people in distress—and if what we *really* feel does not coincide with what we *think* we should be feeling, we get upset. When we are around a dying person, because we feel guilty about how we are reacting, we try to force ourselves to change. But the more we try to make ourselves feel a certain way, the less it works. The result is that we feel bad all the time.

When we are with someone who is dying, we may be surprised to find that we do not feel particularly sad. We might mostly feel inconvenienced or bothered. We might be caught up in our own troubles and resent having to pay attention to someone else. We might be annoyed that we are stuck picking up the ball as our flaky relatives ignore their own family obligations. There is no telling how we will react when we are relating to someone who is dying. But due to our guilt, we are afraid to admit how we really feel to ourselves or to anyone else. When our guilt kicks in, we tell ourselves, "I really shouldn't be feeling this way. What's wrong with me? I'm such a bad person." So we try to assuage our guilt and convince ourselves that we don't actually feel the way we do.

When we are caught up in guilt, we begin to resent the people we are trying to help because being with such people reminds us of our own personal shortcomings. That resentment makes us feel even *more* guilty. We try to make up for that guilt by working more and more furiously. We try to *will* ourselves to be compassionate, but this forced approach quickly backfires.

As helpers, nothing we do feels adequate to what we should be doing.

If we need help ourselves, we try to force that as well, by making *other* people feel guilty. But the more demanding we are, the less satisfying is the help we receive. We feel increasingly estranged from the person we have manipulated into helping us. And the more estranged and unsatisfied we feel, the more demanding we become. It is a vicious circle. So when we are not laying guilt trips on ourselves, we lay guilt trips on the people around us.

Heavy-Handed Compassion

The last of the twisted types of compassion is the heavy-handed variety. There is nothing light about this kind of compassion, and there is absolutely no humor. Instead, when we are around someone who is dying, we attempt to create a solemn, heavy, religious atmosphere that is all very hushed and quiet. In such an atmosphere, no one dares to speak above a whisper or say anything less than profound.

In guilt-based compassion, we tried to make our feelings conform to our expectations. In heavy-handed compassion, we try to manipulate the tone of the whole environment. We want to ensure that everyone involved is aware of the meaningfulness and significance of the occasion. Lights are dimmed, soft music is playing, everyone is trying his or her best to demonstrate piety and profound concern. It is all so earnest. The atmosphere is positively dripping with meaning.

The problem is, the atmosphere we've created is also stifling. We can only maintain it by keeping a heavy lid on everyone's behavior. We strictly censure anything that does not fit our scheme. It is obvious that we take that task very seriously—we take *ourselves* very seriously. Eventually we become completely caught up in our own importance. We are so attached to the solemn atmosphere we have established that we are insulted if there is the slightest disturbance. Freshness, spontaneity, humor, lack of pretension, foibles, and flaws are all seen as threats.

COMPASSION IS A TRICKY THING. It is tempting to cloak our fear and self-centeredness in the guise of compassion, like a wolf in sheep's clothing. In that way, we *seem* to be compassionate, but we need not expose too much of ourselves or take the risk of extending ourselves to another person. We can try to have compassion without pain. The problem is that when we mask our own vulnerability, we mask the wellspring of naturally arising compassion that is our nature. Although that compassion can easily be distorted by fear and self-concern, it can also be a force drawing us beyond our usual limitations.

The activity of compassion arises from the recognition of our interconnectedness with one another and our natural impulse to help. True compassion is like the sun, which effortlessly radiates warmth. The sun does not choose who is or is not worthy of receiving sunlight—it shines on everyone. Neither does the sun check for results or seek confirmation. For the sun, shining is not a project, nor is the sun on a mission of mercy. Nonetheless, through its warmth, the entire earth is nourished. The sun is already in the sky. We don't have to worry about putting it there; we simply need to remove the clouds that block us from seeing it.

When we try to be of help and act with compassion in real-life situations, such as when a friend is sick or dying, we are put to the test. We see that moments of genuine compassion are mixed in with distorted versions of compassion we manufacture out of our own fear. The more we work with our compassion, the more clearly we see the contrast between distorted compassion and the genuine article.

In order to develop compassion, we need not wait until we are perfect and our actions are untainted. That might take a very long time. What we can do is put ourselves in situations in which we are pushed to be compassionate and see what happens. That is how we learn about our own style of compassion and the obstacles that come up for us personally. When we do so, we have the opportunity to push beyond our fear. Each time we extend ourselves even a little bit, we create more room for genuine compassion to take root.

GIVING AND RECEIVING HELP

Sit quietly and let your mind settle.

Think about an occasion when you are called upon for help. What is your own personal style of helping? What obstacles arise for you? What are your personal strengths? When you help another, what distinguishes your experience of genuine compassion from distorted compassion?

Think about an occasion when you need to receive help from others. What is your own personal style of receiving help? What makes it possible for you to accept help? What obstacles get in the way of that? What do you notice about those who are tying to help you? How do you know when you are receiving genuine compassion as opposed to distorted compassion?

From giving help, what can you learn about receiving help? From receiving help, what can you learn about giving help?

To conclude, sit quietly for a few minutes.

Fruition

Helping the Dying

SO FAR, we have been talking about our personal relationship with death and the experience of change generally. We have done a number of exercises and meditation practices that help us deepen our understanding of change and prepare to face death with courage and equanimity. We have introduced the idea of cultivating compassion and some tools for doing so.

Part Three is about caring for the dying, whether we are spending time with a friend or relative or we work as professional caregivers. We will examine how to apply our understanding, compassion, and meditative training in the midst of real-life encounters with dying people. We are taking what we have learned and putting it to practical use.

As a support for being with the dying, I will introduce six basic "slogans." Slogans are pithy statements that encapsulate a larger body of teachings. We can use these six slogans as reminders for continuing to develop awareness and kindness in our work with the dying. They are guidelines that can help us reconnect with the dying person over and over and not lose heart.

We will discuss the importance of the initial connection we make with the dying person and the people surrounding him, from the moment we first walk through the door of his room. Once we have made that initial connection, by paying attention to our own state of mind and the environment around us, we can find many ways to be of help and avoid common obstacles to good care.

The six slogans are valuable guideposts for working with the dying. They can help us deepen our understanding and develop confidence. But they are only pointers. Eventually we must let go of such supports and trust what happens.

13

Reminders

WHEN WE ARE FACING DEATH or working with dying people, the more our actions are grounded in awareness and kindness, the more effective they will be. However, for most of us, that grounding does not come automatically; it has to be developed. That is the purpose of practices such as mindfulness meditation, the contemplation of death, and tonglen. When we are learning to play the piano, if we don't invest some energy in practicing, we might be able to imagine ourselves playing a tune, but actually pulling it off will be difficult. Working with meditation is no different. In the same way that we practice any other skill and, by practicing, gradually get better at it, we can practice being more aware and openhearted and, over time, get better at *that*.

We have a lot to learn, and we need a lot of practice. However, although we may not feel at all ready, at some point we have to take what we have learned and put it to use. We need to test our understanding in real situations. As we go about our daily lives, no matter what we are facing, we could take the attitude of a student. Then, even in difficult times, such as when we are sick or dying or when we are with dying people, we could make use of what we experience to deepen our understanding and to develop greater awareness and kindness. Taking the attitude of a student transforms the way we deal with difficulties generally. Instead of just trying to grit our teeth and push through, we keep our curiosity and inquisitiveness intact. So although we are struggling, at the same time we are always learning.

When we are under pressure and caught up with our own concerns, it is easy to lose our ability to learn from experience. Although we may be doing more and more, we seem to be learning less and less. How do we reconnect with what we are doing and infuse our actions with greater awareness and kindness? How do we extend our practice of mindfulness and tonglen to help someone who is dying? If we cannot apply what we have learned, our good intentions, study, and training will be of little benefit to anyone but ourselves. It is clear that we need more than just theoretical understanding. Day by day, as we go about our lives, we need to apply ourselves to putting our understanding into practice. As my meditation teacher so succinctly put it, "Words don't cook rice."

Trying to join our understanding and our behavior is, of course, an ongoing and difficult project. Without reminders, we are apt to forget about that project completely and operate more on autopilot than on inspiration. The following six slogans are such reminders:

1. Start with knowledge.

2. Give and receive.

3. Pay attention to details.

4. Slow down.

5. Don't give up.

6. Be present.

Over and over, they call our attention to the gap between our desire to express awareness and compassion and our ability to do so—and they give us guidelines for how to bridge that gap. Because of that, we always have something to work with and a way to go forward.

In working with these slogans, we are deliberately cultivating greater awareness and compassion in all our actions. In particular, we are cultivating the ability to help other people more effectively, especially those who are sick or dying. Hopefully, over time, the need for deliberate effort will fade as we become able to manifest these same qualities spontaneously.

Helping others is a journey with no end point, and the way each of us goes about that journey is unique. The road we are traveling is not a smooth one, nor is it well marked, and along the way, we lose track again and again. Sometimes we have to double back; sometimes we need to take detours. There are no clear maps. The only trustworthy guides are our own awareness and self-knowledge. Only we ourselves know when we have lost our way and when we have regained it, when we are fully engaged in our world and when we have pulled back. The six slogans are reminders to pay attention to our own insight.

When we feel discouraged and trapped, inadequate and confused, whatever trouble is before us seems to fill our entire world. We lose track of who we are and have no sense of moving forward. Yet hopeless as it may seem, sometimes all it takes is a reminder to free us from that small, stuck world and restore a bigger perspective.

The six slogans interrelate and balance one another. They alternate like the inbreath and the outbreath. The first slogan, "Start with knowledge," is a reminder of the importance of study and training, gathering information, learning. But we can't just keep preparing forever; we need to apply that knowledge. We must make decisions and act. In the second slogan, "Give and receive," we are entering the realm of action. This slogan is about interacting with others in a balanced way so that as we extend out to other people, at the same time, we are accepting what they have to offer us. In that way, we are continuously extending out and expanding our horizons and encouraging that same breadth of mind in the people with whom we are dealing.

In our expansiveness, we could get carried away and fail to notice the many nuances of what is going on right in front of us. The third slogan, "Pay attention to details," brings us back to immediate, concrete, nitty-gritty reality. But we could get caught up in the meticulous world of endless details. Trying to keep track of it all could make us frantic. The next slogan, "Slow down," cuts that speed. It is about letting things happen at their own pace. However, that slowing-down process could veer into laziness. We could become too lackadaisical. An infusion of effort is necessary. The slogan "Don't give up" is a reminder that without hard work, we won't be of much help to anyone. It is about not backing down from the hard work of helping.

When we exert ourselves, we may push too hard and take ourselves much too seriously. We could become earnest and uptight and so fixated on trying to make something happen that we are constantly discouraged when things don't go our way. Our exertion is no longer that helpful if we are unable to stop. As a counterbalance, we need the last slogan, "Be present," to remind us of the power of simple presence, silence, and stillness.

If we take the attitude that whatever we face has the possibility of teaching us something, then whatever we encounter has value. The six slogans give us a way to bring out that value, even in the most difficult of circumstances. A dance teacher I met in Bali had ongoing health problems and a bad stomach, yet he kept up a very busy schedule. When I was talking to him about this, he smiled broadly and told me, "It is not so hard to keep working because even though I am very busy, I am never lonely. I never go anywhere without my four closest companions: sickness, aging, pain, and death." He had found a way to value his difficulties as well as his good fortune. In facing our own hardships, and in facing death and the many other difficult transitions that come up in our lives, we could do the same.

Working with the slogans is based on no longer separating ourselves from our world but always bringing our personal experience into the equation. As we work with others, we are always at the same time working with ourselves. It is a two-way street: being a teacher is a way to learn; being a healer is a way of being healed. We are fooling ourselves if we think that we can check our personal thoughts, reactions, and habits at the door and assume some new identity when we go about working with others, whether that identity be professional caregiver, doting friend, or saint.

If we suppress who we are and take on such a pseudoidentity, we distance ourselves from what we are doing. Gradually we become more and more numb and insensitive. In the short run, we may feel some relief from the pain of working with the sick and dying, but we will pay for it in the long run. A doctor I know told me that studies have shown that medical professionals who try to protect themselves from the pain they encounter by shutting down their normal human feelings pay later through ill health and shortened life spans. Distancing strategies have a heavy price tag.

We must find ways to link knowledge and action, to see what needs to be done and do it skillfully. We must find ways to apply our past experience and training to whatever is immediately in front of us. The six slogans can help us do so, but they are merely pointers. If someone tries to show us something by pointing her finger, once we figure out what she is pointing at, that pointing finger is no longer necessary. Likewise, no matter how helpful the slogans may be, it would be a mistake to rely on them like recipes. At some point, we must set them aside and move on.

The six slogans point to how we might work with our own behavior patterns in order to engage more skillfully and intelligently with our world. But each situation is complex and unique. Our experience cannot be crammed into a box, no matter how good a box it may be. Pointers can be helpful, but fundamentally, we are on our own, and every experience is fresh and challenging. In fact, that is exactly what is being pointed out. So in the end, we must learn to trust and rely on our own innate insight. The slogans point beyond themselves. They are designed to self-destruct as we reduce our reliance on established strategies and preset answers and begin to open to each new situation as it arises.

14

Start with Knowledge

ALTHOUGH THERE ARE MANY KINDS of knowledge, four basic types are most relevant in the present context: outer knowledge, self-knowledge, attentiveness, and intuition. When we are working with someone who is sick or dying, outer knowledge includes such things as the nature of the disease and its effects, treatment options, pain control, the rights of the patient, the workings of the bureaucracies with which we are dealing, and the nature of the support group of friends or relatives. Self-knowledge is understanding who we are and what we have to offer, our strengths and weaknesses. Attentiveness means being alert and observant, able to pick up on what is happening and learn from it. Intuitive knowledge is deep knowledge that bubbles up like a spring. It can appear as a flash of insight or in the images of a dream. The practice of this slogan is to bring together all four types of knowledge in order to get a more complete view of whatever is going on.

OUTER KNOWLEDGE

In dealing with sickness or death — or anything else, for that matter — it obviously helps to have some literal knowledge of what is going on and what to expect. In other words, we need to do our homework and not just wing it. When we fall sick, it can seem as if we have involuntarily signed up for a crash course in topics we previously had not the slightest interest in, such as where the pancreas is located and what it does. We are expected to assimilate all this new material and make life-and-death decisions in an atmosphere in which there is both too much and too little information—too much information to absorb or digest quickly and not enough information to know for sure what to do.

We face all kinds of decisions when we are dealing with someone who is dying, such as whether further treatment makes sense, whether he needs to be hospitalized or can stay at home, and what options are covered by his insurance plan. There are legal issues we must understand. For instance, what are a person's rights if he is sick or on the verge of death? How much authority do we have in the event that we want to change or discontinue his treatment? What did the dying person want us to do in the event that he became incapacitated?

After a death has occurred, there are additional things we need to know. Whom should we contact? If we want to have a funeral ceremony or keep someone's body at home undisturbed for three or four days, what would it take to do that? What kind of funeral did the dying person want? Did she want to be cremated or buried? Did she want her body donated to a medical school? To negotiate our way through all this, we need plain, ordinary information and advice. This is the first kind of knowledge.

Sometimes the search for knowledge can become obsessive. We think that if we do enough research, we might find a way around death altogether. We are afraid to face the burden of responsibility for making life-and-death decisions when "all the facts are not in." We can't accept that all the facts may *never* be in.

More often, we don't gather enough knowledge. When my friend's grandmother died recently, after a prolonged illness, not a single person in her family had a clue as to how she had wanted her death to be handled. So many critical questions remained unanswered: Was the woman even aware that she was dying? Did she want aggressive treatment if she began to fail? Did she prefer to die in the hospital or at home? Did she want to be cremated or buried? Since she had not been particularly religious and disliked ceremonies in general, did she even want a funeral? This kind of knowledge does not emerge easily or automatically. It must be gathered, which requires that we overcome our hesitation and start talking about such difficult topics. Unless we address such issues, we will remain in the dark.

SELF-KNOWLEDGE

When we are working with the dying or facing our own death, along with outer knowledge, it is important to know ourselves, both our strengths and our weaknesses. What personal strengths can we rely on? What really sets us off? What we do when we are on the verge of being overwhelmed and totally losing it? What happens to our mindfulness and kindness under such circumstances? What is our state of mind *then*? When things are not going smoothly, how do we react? We need to know.

Developing self-knowledge means becoming familiar with how we handle difficulties. By examining how we have conducted ourselves in the past, we can learn from our experience. We can be in touch with our own strengths and weaknesses. If we are realistic about our limitations and do not try to hide them, we have a base for working with others honestly and realistically. For instance, some people literally can't stand the sight of blood; it actually makes them pass out. If that is the case, you might be better off helping behind the scenes or dropping a dying friend a note rather than visiting. If we are aware of what triggers us to anger or frustration, we can catch ourselves before it is too late.

We can avoid becoming a cause of disruption rather than a source of help. We know when to stay and when to leave.

Self-knowledge means that we dig deeply enough to achieve an honest and deep-seated understanding of ourselves. Outer knowledge is about developing our understanding of the experience of death and dying, and the circumstances that surround it. When we are with someone who is dying, outer knowledge includes learning about who that person is and what kind of care he or she wants. Both outer knowledge and self-knowledge are essential to working with dying people effectively.

ATTENTIVENESS

Attentiveness is being open to new input from the environment around us. It is having sensitive antennae that pick up on what is going on. Fortunately, it is possible to sharpen our antennae with practice. Years ago, I was chosen to direct the Naropa Institute (now Naropa University) in Boulder, Colorado. This appointment came as a surprise to me, totally out of the blue, especially since I did not have much knowledge or experience in running any organization. Although I got lots of advice from my friends, what proved most helpful had to do with this third type of knowledge. That advice was to spend some time each day "scanning," which simply meant walking through the school with no particular agenda and in an easy and relaxed way picking up on what was happening: the feeling of the place, the energy of the day, the forces at work, the predominant mood, the undercurrents. Scanning in this way enabled me to probe beneath the never-ending complexities at the surface of the organization, all of which seemed to demand attention at once, and find one or two things to do that might actually make a difference and move the school forward.

Similarly, when we encounter death, there are often so

many complexities that we do not know what to do and so much information that we do not know how to sort through it all. So we need to sharpen our antennae in order not to miss what is important. Scanning is a way to figure out "what is really going on." It is a way to open ourselves to fresh knowledge.

INTUITIVE KNOWLEDGE

Intuitive knowledge is a free-flowing kind of knowledge. It doesn't come from you or from the person you're with; it emerges spontaneously, seeming to arise from the space between you. It sometimes appears in images or dreams. We could call it knowledge that comes from nowhere—a flash of intuition or insight in which we suddenly know something we didn't realize we knew before. It is not a knowledge we can acquire; it is a knowledge that only shows up if there is room for it. To contact that direct intuitive understanding, we must quiet down.

When my friend Peter was dying, the people around him were concerned because he did not seem to be relating with it. There was a lot of discussion about how to get him to face up to the reality that he only had a short time left. He was a brilliant man, so how could he ignore the obvious? When anybody brought up the possibility of death, he would argue with him or her or just clam up, so nobody talked about it. Then one day, when we were just sitting around doing nothing, Peter asked for a mirror. After looking carefully at his image for some time, he turned to me and asked, "Tell me the truth. How do I look? Do I look that bad?" I tried to be honest and simply describe what I saw in front of me: "You look terrible. You remind me of an inmate in a concentration camp." He consulted the mirror again and said, "You're right. It looks like I am dying." His recognition was immediate. There was an opening, and the time was ripe— and that was all it took.

Another friend had once had breast cancer but had shown no signs of it for many years. When she discovered a small lump, she was quite frightened that her cancer had spread. The night that she went into the hospital for her surgery, I awoke in the middle of the night from a nightmare in which I was traveling up a long spiral ramp to my execution. This ramp had three loops, and I knew that I would not die at the end of the first loop or the second, but at the end of the third I would be face-to-face with the executioner. As I reached this third loop, I awoke in a sweat, completely terrified. Somehow, at that moment, I knew this meant that my friend's cancer would strike her three times, and that the first two times, she would recover and the third time she would not. The next day, when the lump was removed, her doctors told her the recurrence was very localized and a full recovery was likely. However, three years later, the cancer came back, and within a short time, she was dead. It was unusual for me to trust a dream in this way, although I have heard many stories from ordinary people like myself of times when knowledge emerged in like fashion, through imagery and imagination.

IN THE FIRST SLOGAN, "Start with knowledge," we begin by learning what we can about what is going on and how we can work with that. But outer knowledge by itself is just partial knowledge; it is only about what is "out there." It is equally important to develop self-knowledge, to understand what is going on "in here," whether we are the caregiver or the one who is sick. When we know and accept ourselves, we begin to relax. This enables us to sharpen our antennae and develop greater attentiveness. Finally, the combination of relaxation and attentiveness creates an opening for direct intuitive insight.

15

Give and Receive

THE SECOND SLOGAN is about generosity. When we are with someone who is dying, we are at the most basic level simply sharing space with another person. We are extending ourselves beyond our own private sphere, and we are inviting another person in. Sharing has to do with offering something of ourselves and—*equally important*—accepting what the other person is offering us. We are giving and receiving, extending out and inviting in, continually. As our sense of shared ground increases, our territoriality and defensiveness decrease. We expand our view and include more and more. This expansive atmosphere makes it possible for us to open our world and include others fully.

When we do give, there are many ways to give and many types of gifts. We can give material objects, comfort and support, the gift of honest communication—whatever is needed. No matter what we give, or how much we give, by the act of giving itself, we are cultivating an attitude of generosity. In the Tibetan culture, a basic metaphor for generosity is the custom of offering a white scarf. Traditionally, when you first meet with someone, you express your respect by offering that person the gift of a white scarf. Immediately upon receiving the scarf, the recipient in turn offers that same scarf back to you. Over time, you might offer that scarf again and again, and each time you give it away, it is given right back to you. So over and over, you are practicing how to give and receive cleanly. Offering a white scarf is a metaphor for how the attitude of continually giving and receiving links us with one another.

When we give and receive, giver and receiver are on equal ground. One is not higher or lower than the other. Generosity is an exchange, not a one-way street. Generosity connects us with each other, whether we are the giver or the receiver, and enriches us both. However, it is possible to give and receive without really being generous at all. We may appear to care about people, but our real interest is in benefiting ourselves. We use generosity as a means of controlling people or bringing them under our sphere of influence, like bribery. It is like the generosity of parents who shower their children with gifts, trying to buy their love and affection, or the generosity of a suitor who figures that with the right gift, the payoff is to be invited to spend the night. Rather than being an exchange, we are using our pretense of generosity to increase our own richness by depleting the other person's.

As receivers, we may also act with false generosity by trying to take advantage of someone else and playing on his or her weakness and guilt. We nag and nag, and mournfully muse, "Oh, I really wish I could have that. Too bad nobody realizes how much I would like it. It would make me so happy." Eventually we might succeed in weaseling out the gift we seek through such guilt-tripping. But since that gift was given grudgingly, not freely, it is not fully satisfying. It is packaged in the resentment that comes from being manipulated.

It does not matter whether someone is helping us or asking us for our help—either way, we cringe. Hearing the words "Oh, you poor thing. May I help you?" makes us want to run away and hide. No one wants to be pitied. It benefits only the pitier. Being drawn in to help someone through his or her display of whining and duplicitousness is equally unsatisfactory. In either case, we feel creepy, belittled, manipulated, used. We are not making a true connection but simply using people. Giving and receiving in that way is not enriching either party but impoverishing both. There is no balance and no real exchange taking place. In contrast, true generosity feels liberating. It is a relief to be able to give freely and spontaneously; and when we receive help from another, we feel appreciated and accepted, not belittled.

If we look into our own experience with generosity, on either the giving or the receiving end, we can feel the difference between false and true generosity. Some ways of giving are clean and straightforward; others are manipulative and self-serving. Sometimes we feel a bond, a common ground of connection, and we both feel richer from the encounter. Other times we feel depleted by giving and belittled by receiving. Practicing this slogan helps us explore the nature of generosity in order to learn how to give and receive cleanly.

The starting point of generosity is simply opening ourselves to others. To give or receive, we first need to allow others into our world. This means seeing them as people who exist independently of us, people in their own right apart from whatever they are doing for us specifically. Many people are invisible; they don't matter to us. As far as we are concerned, they are background. You can see how this works if you think about going to the grocery store and having your purchases rung up. How do you relate to the cashier? Do you see a person or a faceless receipt giver? My daughter told me that when she worked as a cashier, although people looked at her, they did not see her at all. It was as though she were a machine or an attachment to the cash register.

It is easy to be so absorbed in our own worries that we don't notice other people, let alone see their worries as important. For most of us, our particular major problem of the moment is the only problem in the whole wide world that really matters. When we visit someone who is sick, for instance, at first glance it may seem as if that person is at the center of everybody's attention, the focus of everyone's care. But when we look closer, we find that the patient is not at the center at all but functions as background. He has become a prop in a melodrama that does not even include him as a central character. In such a scene, everybody around the sick or dying person is completely entranced by his or her own mental drama. This one is pissed that she had to take time off from work; that one is about to start sobbing because he feels so sad; another one is distracted and bored and wondering how long it's going to take. Everybody is swirling around in his or her own concerns—and meanwhile, as an almost invisible presence, there is the sick person lying there creating all this drama. That is what happens when people fail to see beyond their own preoccupations.

When we are absorbed in our personal concerns, we lose contact with anything outside them. We lose connection with the presence of the person in front of us. That just goes out the window. When we notice ourselves losing connection with others, we could practice shifting our perspective outward and putting aside our internal preoccupations for the time being. In the same way that we bring our attention back to the breath in meditation practice, we could bring our attention back to the dying person. We could once again recognize the presence of that person as an individual who has her own reality separate from us. Something is happening outside us and our little mind and our personal concerns. There's a bigger world, even if at first it only stretches a few feet in front of us. That is important ground to come back to again and again. We will find ourselves losing that ground in so many ways, but each time, we can bring ourselves back and again feel the presence of the other person. Once we do so, we can see what signals the dying person is putting out and open up the possibility of giving and receiving.

We lay the groundwork for generosity by inviting other people into our world or by letting our own world go for a while and entering the world of another. In both cases, we are extending beyond our own small world. We are willing to include others, and we are willing to be included. When we have expanded our perspective in that way, we can give and receive with fewer strings attached. If we are sick or dying, we may be embarrassed to be on the receiving end of people's generosity. We may feel guilty about being sick. Although we consider ourselves generous and like to *give* gifts to others, we may find it hard to *accept* gifts from others. We like to help but are uncomfortable being helped. However, that attitude is a form of stinginess, for not accepting what others offer us cuts off communication and undermines *their* generosity. It is an expression of richness, not poverty, to be able to receive help from others.

Sometimes it is better to receive than to give. Someone who is sick or dying may feel that he has nothing to offer and that when he does try to offer something, no one cares to receive it—apart from an inheritance, of course. For someone who feels he is only taking from others, to be acknowledged for what he is providing the people around him is a great gift. So if we are visiting someone who is dying, the most generous thing to do might be to accept and acknowledge what we are receiving from that person rather than thinking of what we might have to give him. In my father's last days, I received many gifts from him. One of the most poignant was his recollection of a single beautiful fall day years before when we had driven to Wisconsin to buy apples. La Crescent apples were in season, and they were crisp and delicious. They made great fresh cider, too. In his telling of this story, my father captured a moment in time that was ordinary and perfect. He offered that story as a gift, and in accepting that gift, I felt welcomed into his world and enriched by it.

A Buddhist scripture tells us that generosity is the virtue that produces peace. How? By dissolving the roadblocks we build based on our own stinginess—our emotional, ideological, and material stinginess. Because generosity is expansive in nature, it undercuts the more narrow approach of holding grudges, clinging to anger, and territoriality. It is like a laxative for psychic constipation. For some people, an encounter with death is the catalyst that draws them out of their stinginess and frees them from the pain that it causes. A woman I met recently lost her husband to AIDS. Years ago, when he informed her that he had contracted the virus, and she discovered that she, too, was infected, she swore that she would never forgive him for doing that to her. She just couldn't do it. Although they remained together as a couple, the burden of guilt and resentment remained, too. But as her husband lay dying, and she saw that time was running out, she could no longer stand the pain of holding on to her resentment toward him. After all those years, she was able to offer her husband her forgiveness. The moment she did so, her husband's demeanor changed completely, and this woman felt a tremendous sense of release from the burden she had carried for so long. Shortly after being forgiven, her husband died. It was as if he had been trying to hold on in hopes of forgiveness, and once he received it, he could finally let go.

In contrast, a student of mine described the incredible pain of seeing his dying grandfather and his father so stuck in a grudge they had carried against each other for years, a grudge that had split the family apart, that they each refused to budge. As his grandfather's death approached, despite the pain of estrangement in the family and the whole family's longing for reconciliation, neither of them would make the first move. When his grandfather died, my student saw that hope for reconciliation dashed forever. The pain of that lost opportunity continues to haunt him. In the face of death, some people are able to extend their generosity in ways that were not possible for them before — but others will carry their stinginess with them to the grave rather than give in.

Even a small thing such as offering an ice chip or listening to a story is an expression of generosity. It need not be some grand gesture. Maybe just showing up and spending time is our gift. However we express our generosity, the exchange of giving and receiving opens things up. When we are stingy, we can actually feel ourselves shrinking and compressing; but if we take even the smallest step in the direction of generosity, we begin to soften and relax. Generosity is loose and open. The more we give and the more we accept, the more rich and expansive we feel. Through the practice of giving and receiving, we participate in a continual exchange with others.

16

Pay Attention to Details

IN LIVING AND IN DYING BOTH, there are many details to attend to. No matter how knowledgeable or generous we may be, if we do not respect these details, we will not be very effective when we try to be of help. It is not that we all have to become "detail men"—so caught up in small issues that we miss the big picture—but the first slogan's overview (the importance of knowledge) and the second slogan's expansiveness (giving and receiving) need to be grounded in concrete activities.

Through small gestures, we can make a big difference, but to know what gestures to make, we need to pay attention to the details of the environment around the dying person and the effects of those details. This includes the immediate physical environment as well as the social and emotional environment. Something as simple as opening a window or picking up the phone can be a big help. When we fail to pay sufficient attention to ordinary physical details, we can do a lot of damage. For instance, a friend of mine was hospitalized a few years ago with Guillain-Barré disease. While he was hooked up to a respirator and unable to move at all, he received a visitor who was extremely friendly and solicitous. The visitor failed to notice one small but crucial detail, however: he was standing on the oxygen hose. Since my friend was paralyzed, there was no way he could signal his visitor to move. Fortunately, the visitor did lift his foot off the hose in time—but merely by chance, not because he had noticed what he was doing.

How we work with details affects the people around us—for better or for worse. For instance, if we are setting up a living room, we begin with a bare room. We may have some idea of the atmosphere we want to create, but that only begins to materialize as we work with the details. As we decide what color to paint the walls, where to put the couch and the table, what pictures to hang—eventually the room starts to come together. Then, when people enter that room, they are affected by what we have done. Regardless of whether they consciously notice the various components of the decor, they can feel that room's harmony or disharmony. All those small decisions have combined to create an entire effect. The environments in which we find ourselves affect us more than we usually realize or acknowledge. By working with our environments in all their details, we can make use of those details to communicate quite powerfully to others.

In our society, many people face their last days in a hospital setting. Hospital rooms are designed for the convenience of the medical staff and to accommodate the machinery and equipment of high-tech medicine. Such rooms are inhabited not by people but by body parts and diseases that need fixing. If a person can't be fixed, she doesn't quite fit in. In such a setting, it is hard to avoid the message that death is a medical event. We could counteract the sterility of that view by bringing in objects that have meaning for the dying person. Within the limitations of the clinical setting, we could incorporate elements that personalize her room. For some people, this might mean bringing in family photos or artwork. For others, it might involve setting up a small shrine or putting up pictures from their spiritual tradition. I have found that when people make small gestures to humanize the hospital room, and bring in objects that convey something about the person inhabiting that room, it has an effect on everyone who enters. It makes it easier for the hospital staff to look beyond medical efficiency alone and relate to the human being lying in the bed. It also helps the dying person link her current experience to her life as a whole and its meaning.

Working with details includes the very personal and ordinary level of everyday decency. By our demeanor, gestures, speech, and dress, we demonstrate our appreciation and respect for one another. That is the origin of manners: respect and appreciation. So you could say respecting details includes being well mannered. In the hospital setting, this is easily lost. For example, when I was in the hospital with my husband, who was extremely ill but not unconscious, here is how it would often go: A doctor would walk into the room without introducing himself or saying hello to either me or my husband. Then he would look at the machines, check the chart, and start talking to me, ignoring the presence of my husband completely. Finally, he would hurry out the door to the next patient. Occasionally, a doctor would know how to come into the room and, in the same short time, greet my husband and me, introduce himself, make a brief personal connection, check the machines, and leave. The difference was not in the amount of time each doctor spent. It was not a matter of time but a question of respect. Through the details of their behavior, two doctors could create entirely different atmospheres in that hospital room in a matter of minutes.

The details of our behavior may seem insignificant, but they reflect our basic attitude toward the people around us. If we distinguish between people who are sick and those who are healthy, or between people who are able and those who are handicapped, it shows in our behavior. All too often, people who are unable to speak clearly, keep clean, or dress themselves are no longer deemed worthy of simple respect on an equal footing with healthy folks. A friend of mine who has MS and is confined to a wheelchair travels frequently with her husband. The people they encounter on these trips tend to avoid dealing with her directly and instead direct all their communication to her through her husband. And when they do address her, they talk down to her, a brilliant philosopher, as though she were a child. Yet it is doubtful whether such people are at all aware of what they are doing and its effect. The slogan "Pay attention to details" is about looking into the details of our behavior and seeing how they reflect underlying attitudes that we may not be aware of, how they reinforce such attitudes, and what they communicate to others.

This slogan also has to do with the power of small gestures. When we are working with dying people, our best way to communicate may be through something as simple as combing someone's hair, washing his or her face, or tucking in a sheet. The way in which we do these simple things can convey respect and appreciation or, conversely, disrespect and annoyance. Our gestures can be empty or full; they can serve to connect us with, or distance us from, one another. Our gestures reflect our attitudes. So the smallest gestures have power, they matter, and they affect the environment as a whole. They can make the environment feel nurturing and healing or harsh and impersonal.

Community support can be invaluable. As in the motto "It takes a village to raise a child," you could also say that it takes a village to help people die. When someone is terminally ill, it is helpful to set up a group support system for that person and her family. The people in such a group can help with the many details of care, volunteering a certain amount of time each week. They can set up a communications network to keep friends and relatives informed about the dying person's condition, so that the family is not constantly fielding phone calls. In that way, they can help protect the immediate family from some of the noise and chaos that inevitably accompany the experience of death in our culture. Volunteers can also take on some of the physical work, such as cooking, cleaning, and running errands. They can help uplift the environment with flowers, artwork, music, and friendly conversation. They can read to the dying person or join her in her meditation practice. Such volunteers may have no particular task other than to be present and available on a regular basis. When little details like these are attended to, it shows. You can feel the care and attention immediately when you enter the environment.

Paying attention to details also applies to working with our own state of mind and energy. It involves deciding both what to do and, equally important, what *not* to do. So it is not about always keeping busy and fussing around. Details are endless. and it is possible to deplete our energy trying to deal with them all and burn out. If we are overburdened, it may be more beneficial in the long run to take a break and replenish our energy rather than try to keep plugging away out of sheer stubbornness. Even a short break to gather perspective and regroup can make a big difference.

The discipline of paying attention to details means being as completely in touch as possible with what we are doing while we are doing it. It can be difficult when we are relating to one person after another to give our full attention to each person we encounter. Inevitably our attention wanders. So in practicing this slogan, we repeatedly bring ourselves back to present experience and the person in front of us. How do we bring ourselves back? First, we must notice that we *are* distracted or spaced-out; then, when we *do* notice, we reconnect with the present moment—over and over again. The discipline is to come back to what is happening, even if it is difficult to face. Instead of mentally checking out and closing down whenever we do not want to deal with something, we bring ourselves back.

If we are sick ourselves or we are working with someone who is sick or dying, how we deal with the details is important. Even a small detail can transform the environment for the better. We can change an environment that is speedy, harsh, and per-functory—in which it is difficult for people to connect with one another—into a healthy, nurturing atmosphere. By doing this, we can affect how people within that environment feel, how they behave, and how they relate to one another. Working with details is like using a fulcrum—a small push here and something big happens over there. So through a small gesture, even something as simple as opening a window, we can make a real difference.

The slogan "Pay attention to details" is about first noticing details and then working with them. Working with the details is a concrete way to make a big difference through a small gesture. The challenge is finding the gesture that matters, out of the many possible choices, and using that gesture to create a more healing environment. Such a healing environment doesn't spring out of thin air in full bloom; we actually have to create it—and to create it, we work with the details.

17

Slow Down

WHEN WE ARE WORKING with the dying, paying attention to details is important. But that attention to details may become too obsessive. In our attempt to keep track of minutiae, we could get more and more frantic. That is where the fourth slogan, "Slow down," comes in. It cuts that speed.

This slogan is about patience. Being patient means that we are willing to slow down and not always push for results. It begins with ourselves, because it is difficult to be patient with others if we are impatient with ourselves. When we are impatient with ourselves, we try to force ourselves to be what we are not. As a result, we are increasingly exasperated with who we are. Because we feel bad about our limitations, we try to ignore them and bully our way through. And when that fails, we get more and more angry. It is a vicious circle. The more we try to force things along, the angrier we get. In this hurry-up, hurry-up mode, any obstacle sparks an outburst. Impatience leads directly to anger.

How do we interrupt this cycle? By slowing down. Patience can be developed; it is not simply that we have it or we don't and that's that. At the same time, patience cannot be forced. Trying to make ourselves be more patient would be just a continuation of the same vicious circle. The practice of patience is based on slowing down and allowing time for things to develop. It is not that we are lazy or have just given up on ourselves; it is that we develop a realistic assessment of who we are as well as some humor about our pretensions. We can relax our state of mind on the spot by being kind to ourselves through patience.

Slowing down even a little, cutting away just a small layer of mental speed, makes a difference. The more our mind is rushing, the less able we are to take in anything new. As Alexander Pope pointed out, "Some people will never learn anything for this reason, because they understand everything too soon." When we are spinning so fast, we cannot see beyond our own narrow assumptions. We reduce the boundaries of what is possible or knowable. Out of fear, we limit what we allow ourselves to think or feel. Anything that does not fit within our restricted parameters of the acceptable is shot down the instant it rears its head.

If we slow down, we open ourselves to new possibilities. Sometimes we push and push trying to figure something out. We try to put all the pieces together and uncover some pattern. We keep working at it, but nothing gels. Finally, we give up and go to bed. Oddly, when we wake up the next morning, we find that the solution is clear, as though the problem had solved itself. How is that possible? Because we were able to relax our mental speed and allow a new perspective to come through.

Patience creates a sense of safe territory, so we no longer feel we have to hide who we are from ourselves or others. It is like putting the hawk in a cage so that the little gophers can peek out. By developing patience with ourselves, we are also making room for others to express who they are. We are establishing an atmosphere in which no one needs to prove anything. Resistance, denial, hysteria, and resentment can all be allowed to surface and be worked with.

Patience accommodates all sorts of different mental states— confusion, emotional outbursts, sudden embarrassing moments—our own and others'. My friend Peter suffered from AIDS-related dementia. In the weeks before his death, he alternated between lucidity and all sorts of emotional and hallucinatory realms. One day, he wondered why we were feeding him wood. Another day, he commented that it was strange that everyone was suddenly speaking German. One day, he would be filled with anger; another day, he would be very calm. Rather than trying to even out his experience, or push Peter to be more logical, the people around him decided just to maintain a steady, supportive presence throughout. In the process, we learned that communication is not limited to what is easily accessible and understood. It happens in a variety of marvelous ways—through hallucinatory imagery, dialogue, silence, physical gestures, raw emotionality. To realize that, we had to slow down and look around without being so quick to judge. Instead of censoring our experience, we were learning to slow down enough to see what was happening.

When we are working with dying people, it is important not to push them to take on the reality and responsibilities of death more quickly than they are able. Because *we* are impatient, we may want the dying person to move along—for our sake, not his. As relatively healthy people dealing with people who are about to die, we feel a sense of urgency and want to make sure that the dying person relates to his remaining time properly. We want that person to take care of whatever remains to be done in his life right away because he has so little time left. There is no time for that person to realize what is going on at his own pace; he has to realize it *right away*—and we will make sure he does! If not, we will try to realize it for him! That is the opposite of patience.

In dealing with people who are seriously ill, slowing down is a way to connect. If we don't slow down, we may be the only ones hearing what we have to say. It does not work to speak at the speed of a rocket when someone is listening at the speed of an oxcart. If we go too fast, we will not be heard, nor will we be able to listen. To a slowed-down person, we will just sound like a chipmunk chattering or a mosquito buzzing around; and when such a person tries to communicate with us, we will be going too fast ourselves to stop and hear her. We will fill in the gap, complete her sentences, try to make sense of things too quickly. But in so doing, we are apt to miss the point. So we have to slow down and simplify in order to connect. We slow down to speak, and we slow down to listen.

I had a meditation student who spent several months at her home, dying of cancer. During this time, she had many helpers and visitors. What I noticed is that many of these visitors, although well-meaning, came around with suggestions and all kinds of advice—on cures, on how to cope with illness, on dying, on how to deal with her mind and psychology. Of course, one person's advice would often conflict with another's. Then, having dispensed their advice, they would want her to respond—to accept the advice or at least engage in a discussion about it. Often she could not follow the long-winded and detailed descriptions of what she should do, but she *did* pick up on the feeling of impatience and of being pressured—and that pressure was wearing her down. Because her visitors were nervous, they could not slow down enough to listen rather than talk at her. So there could be no real dialogue. Their impatience did not solve anything, nor did it fix her situation; it just caused pain. In fact such visits became so draining that she made the decision to allow only visitors who were willing to sit quietly with her and practice mindfulness.

It is hard to be patient. There is such a strong desire to fix things or try to make them better. Instead of letting a painful situation really touch us, we would rather do something— anything—to push away the reality of that pain. Slowing down is a threat because it allows us to feel what is going on. It is tempting to rush through our experience and also hurry the dying person along, and it may seem hard to slow down and relax. But we need to allow time that is not filled with activity, time in which nothing much is happening. We could let events unfold at their own pace. To do so is a great gift, because it allows room for doubt and confusion, room for mistakes. It removes the pressure we feel to uphold pretense and the burden of that pressure on the dying person. In patience, we develop a greater appreciation of the unexpected and feel less need to control the dying process. Ironically, slowing down can open up possibilities that speed and busyness cannot.

18

SLOGAN 5

Don't Give Up

SLOGAN 5 IS ABOUT EFFORT. It is a counterbalance to the previous slogan, "Slow down." Taken to extremes, slowing down can begin to feel more like laziness and an unwillingness to make demands on ourselves. In working with the dying, we need to slow down, but we also need to apply ourselves. This slogan is about effort, work, being willing to expend our energy for others.

The challenge of this slogan is not to give up on the people with whom we are working, not to give up on what we are doing, and not to give up on ourselves. Working with ourselves or with other people involves exertion. And if we are helping someone who is dying, it takes extra effort at a time when our resources may already be depleted. We do not always feel like going out and getting in our car and driving over to the hospital and going into some room and relating with a bunch of crabby relatives. It's too much work. So we think, "Well, maybe I'll just phone the hospital. Or maybe I'll take the night off and watch TV." The effort of working with people—and working with ourselves—is very literal.

When we are around someone who is dying, much of the work that needs to be done is not at all glamorous. The most useful task may be something as simple as running out and buying some food and bringing it back or cleaning the kitchen. We may not always feel like relating to such errands, but it is necessary. In fact, about 99 percent of the time, helping out at the kitchen-sink level is the most useful thing to do. We might prefer to be sitting there basking in our romantic vision of the spiritual experience of the deathbed scene, but it may be better to do the dishes and buy some coffee.

It is easy to have good intentions or think kind thoughts, but actually taking action is another matter altogether. There are so many reasons not to get involved in the first place with someone who is dying or to give up once we do get involved. We are too busy with our own concerns; we lack the energy; we are uncomfortable; we don't know what to say; we don't know how we can help. On the one hand, if we push ourselves and try too hard, we may end up being no help at all because we have burned out. In fact, in the health-care professions, it is the most idealistic, perfectionistic workers who are most vulnerable to burnout. On the other hand, if we try to conserve our energy by not putting too much effort into what we are doing and help out only halfheartedly, we are likely to feel guilty and depressed. In either case, we lose heart. If we are not to lose heart, we need to find a way of working with ourselves and others that involves neither trying too hard nor holding back. In the slogan "Don't give up," we are looking for a middle ground between those two extremes.

Effort is tricky. When a lot is demanded of us, such as when we are working with the dying, we don't always have the energy to deal with it. The intensity of what we are experiencing seems to literally suck the energy out of us, and we feel increasingly depleted. We begin to fear that our energy might run out altogether. As our energy drains away, we try to find some way to get recharged, like an old battery. There are also times when the more that is demanded of us, the more we do, and the more we do, the more energy we have. So although exertion and hard work can deplete our energy, they can also have the opposite effect—further increasing our energy.

It takes very little effort to act when what we are doing appeals to us and make us comfortable, but dealing with a situation we would rather avoid—something challenging, messy, or threatening, like death—takes tremendous energy. The sense of having no energy can be a way of masking the fact that we just do not want to relate with illness and death. Somehow, we have this primitive, magical belief that if we refuse to relate with death, it isn't really happening. When my younger daughter was a small child, she thought that if she covered her ears and closed her eyes and made an ear-piercing noise, whatever she did not want to deal with at the time would disappear. As adults, our avoidance tactics may be more subtle, but we still resist relating to situations we'd rather were not happening. Our resistance is a heavy weight dragging us down. Resistance is the reason why it seems to take twice the energy to deal with the areas of our life we customarily avoid. Where does that resistance come from? It comes from us. It's something that we ourselves add.

Our resistance, our unwillingness to relate to certain aspects of our self and our world, can be expressed in inertia, or it can take the form of being extremely busy and completely preoccupied with our own concerns. For instance, if we are not too tired to relate with death, we are too busy to deal with it. When we are lethargic, we have no energy to do anything useful. When we are buried in our own work, we have no time for anything else. We always have plenty of reasons why we lack the time to deal with death. We justify our noninvolvement and make all sorts of excuses. We keep meaning to help, but it just doesn't happen. It is hard to overcome our resistance to dealing with difficult situations such as illness or death. It is tempting to give up on ourselves and abandon any hope of being of real help.

Resistance is based on a sense of separation between ourselves and the outside world. We create a small zone of personal comfort removed from the demands of the world around us. When that personal comfort zone is threatened, as when we are required to deal with difficult or demanding situations, we feel pressured, even attacked, and we respond by strategizing our retreat, as if we were on a battlefield. In trying to figure out how to avoid dealing with illness and death or how to get out of them or to what extent to respond to them, we bolster our sense of being cut off from the world around us. We feel the weight of responsibility, and we struggle against it.

We do not always get caught up in that struggle. When we find ourselves suddenly thrown into the midst of an urgent situation and have no time to strategize or beat a retreat, the sense of struggle disappears. We feel completely connected with what is happening around us. The sense of separation dissolves, and our effort is not at all strained. Over and over in my classes, people have reported that when they faced life-threatening situations such as a car wreck, an assault, or a battlefield attack, they found that time slowed down, and they seemed to know just what to do to survive. In extremes like that, whatever it is that makes us perceive effort as a burden, as demanding, just falls away, and our actions seem to accomplish themselves.

Such experiences challenge our conventional views of what effort is all about. It is as though once we cross a boundary or step over a divide, and there is no turning back, our energy is liberated. Once we overcome our initial hesitation and resistance, pondering whether to get in or stay out, pondering what to do or how much energy to commit, there is no more second-guessing. When we just jump in, or find ourselves thrust into the middle of things, exertion is a natural response to the immediacy of whatever we are facing. In Buddhist teachings, we talk about "choicelessness." It is tremendously freeing to stop carrying around, somewhere in a nook or cranny of our mind, the possibility of escape. Giving up that option allows us to act with 100 percent conviction. There is no room for resistance because we are fully identified with what we are doing.

Usually we are not in such a heightened state nor so fully

identified with what we are doing, but we can still work to develop a steadier quality of exertion. We could begin by noticing
more precisely where we feel comfortable and not at all challenged and where we feel totally overwhelmed. We could become more clear about our limits. That gives us something to
work with, a way to go forward. Some people need to learn how
to rest and not always push themselves to the point of collapse.
Other people need to learn to push themselves more and overcome their resistance and tendency to hold back.

When we keep pushing ourselves, it is easy to fall into the
trap of being unable to stop. As our energy gets stirred up, it
builds and builds until we are totally tight. Working with the
slogan "Don't give up," we are trying to develop effort that is
steady and reliable and does not deplete itself. A music therapist
I know works with severely ill children at a major hospital in
New York. In this highly demanding job, she often reaches the
point at which she is both stirred up and drained by the intensity
of her work. Her energy runs away from her, and there is no
controlling it. When that happens, the temptation is to keep
pushing, but that only makes it worse. So when she recognizes
this pattern, instead of trying to operate on runaway energy, she
makes the effort to stop cold—if only for a minute or two. She
has found that the best way to replenish her energy is to go off
by herself for a few moments and let her churned-up energy
settle. By taking a short break to let herself digest what has happened, she is able to regroup her energy and make a fresh start.
Not giving up does not mean always pushing ahead; it can also
mean knowing when to stop and start over. As our energy careens
between wired and depleted, if we want to find a steadier thread
of exertion, we may need to do this over and over again.

Our level of exertion varies for many reasons. When we dislike what we are doing or find ourselves working with people
we dislike or who dislike us, it is hard to keep working without
disconnecting psychologically. A student of mine who works

with the elderly in a nursing home talked about a period in his work when every one of his clients was a grumpy old man. It became harder and harder for him to rouse himself to get up and go to work, knowing that what he could expect was nonstop abuse and annoyance. He was rapidly losing heart. He tried to tell himself that he would be like those old men someday, grumpy and in need of help, but that approach didn't seem to work. Finally he had this insight: he didn't have to like everyone with whom he worked, nor did he have to try to *make* himself like them. This discovery enabled him to keep working. He was keenly aware of the pain these men were creating for themselves and those around them; however, since he was no longer personally captured by that pain, he was able to see openings for communication with the men and how he might be of help. At the same time, he began to admit to himself that in some cases, there was nothing he could do to bridge the gap he felt between himself and his clients. It was difficult for him to face up to that, but when he did, he was able to renew his effort and inspiration.

It is important to distinguish straightforward effort from the more heavy-handed and humorless, overly earnest approach. I have a friend who is in and out of a mental hospital. He can be delightful at certain times and demanding and abusive at others. In one encounter, when I had gone out of my way to meet with him, all he did was make demands and complain. I noticed that my immediate reaction was, "Who needs this? I'm out of here. I don't need this kind of abuse. Ingrate!" I could feel the energy and inspiration draining out of me. But in a flash, the ridiculousness of my hope for recognition and its accompanying self-pity was crystal-clear. As soon as I dropped that hope, my energy was back. It was my earnestness that had caused my energy to run out so quickly, and all it took to replenish that energy was a tiny glimpse of humor.

Not giving up means that we find a way to keep going, that we are steady. Sometimes we need to push ourselves, and at other times, we need to rest. Effort is not all or nothing; it is a balance. It is important that we not be afraid to rest, if that is required, and not be afraid to push ourselves, if that is demanded. How do we work with exertion? We do it moment by moment. Working with effort is not a project. We are not trying to talk ourselves into working harder and harder. Instead, we are dealing with each challenge as it arises, seeing where we hold back and where we are pushing too hard. Over and over, we are challenged to use our energy wisely.

Exertion is steady like the gait of an elephant. An elephant moves slowly, but it gets where it wants to go. It is hard to stop an elephant once it is under way. An elephant is tall and can see far into the distance. So small obstacles have little impact. It does not lose sight of where it is going. Like the elephant, when we work with exertion, we are continually moving forward. We never know what will come up from day to day. Some days we are clear; some days we are foggy; some days we are inspired; some days we couldn't care less—we feel all kinds of ways. It is easy to get stuck in whatever we happen to be feeling at the moment. Instead of going forward simply, step-by-step, we are always waiting—waiting for our energy to settle, waiting for our energy to rev up, waiting for the time when we feel just right. The slogan "Don't give up" means that instead of waiting, we work with whatever our energy may be. Since we never know what we will encounter next, we just keep going, one step after another.

19

Be Present

THERE IS A TIME FOR ACTION and a time for nonaction. We need to learn how to distinguish between those two—to know when it is better to do something and when it is more helpful to do nothing. The slogan "Don't give up" is about extending ourselves and working hard. It is about effort. The sixth slogan, "Be present," is about relaxing that effort. It is a way of working with our tendency to get so caught up in our work that we forget what we are trying to accomplish. It is easy to completely lose track of what we are doing and why. That is why it is so important to stop occasionally and remind ourselves to be present.

In our society, we put a lot of emphasis on doing. So it can be frustrating to be in a situation in which there is often not all that much to do, as in relating with the sick or dying. But fundamentally it is our *being* that matters, who we really are and how that manifests in *whatever* we do.

I was talking to a hospice nurse whose work was to visit dying people in their homes. She described how very difficult most people found it to simply be with a dying person at the point when there was no longer any need to administer treatment or any point in doing so. In her opinion, most of the treatments that nurses were requested to give dying people in their final days were not for that person's benefit at all but for the benefit of the people around him or her. One example she gave involved relatives who worried that the dying person was no longer drinking fluids. The hospice nurse found that it made the relatives feel better if she administered liquids intravenously, even after she told them that such fluids would do nothing, as they could no longer be absorbed by someone so close to death. Doing something meaningless was more palatable to that dying person's relatives than doing nothing and letting things take their natural course. Recognizing that, the nurse decided to go through the motions of treatment in order to ease the tension of the deathbed scene.

It is not easy to stop and be present. Our sense of presence, or essential being, is the most powerful gift we can offer, and in turn, we can draw out that quality in others. There is tremendous value in simply being able to sit still and be with another person without pretense. But in our emphasis on doing and on constant activity, we have lost touch with the power of simple presence and the value of nonaction.

Most of the time, even though we may appear to be present on a superficial level, in terms of actual presence, we are not quite there. So simply showing up someplace is not at all the same thing as being present. In grade school, my teachers used to do roll call each morning. When I heard my name, I yelled, "Present!" even though I was anything but.

Being present is not the same thing as simply sitting still either. In fact, we may sit still in order to disappear or be present to the smallest possible extent. For instance, occasionally my teacher would call on a student to deliver a spontaneous discourse. At those times, I worked hard to sit very still and create an invisible shield around me so that I could psychically disappear from view. Instead of expressing my presence, by sitting as still as possible, I was covering it up as much as I could.

The quality of presence is obscured when we are distracted and unsynchronized physically, emotionally, or mentally. My daughter rides horses, and in describing different horses' gaits, she uses the term *collected*. A horse is collected when all its parts move together harmoniously. It is as though the horse were brought into focus and none of its movements were extraneous or disconnected. Physically, the sense of presence is similar to that sense of being collected. There is a quality of stability when we are sitting still, and when we move, we move for a reason. We do not just fidget.

To develop a sense of presence at the body level, we could begin by observing how we habitually handle our body and how that affects us. Are we connected with our body, or does our connection come and go? Are we inhabiting all of it, or are there dead zones? Are we sort of half in and half out, like Swiss cheese? We begin to sense our physical presence or lack of it, and we can observe this in others as well. Being present is not some ethereal state; it begins at this very simple level of reconnecting with and reinhabiting our body.

Our habits of speech can also pull us away from being present. Sometimes we talk just to talk, for no particular reason. When we are nervous, we may try to soothe that sensation by chattering. Speech is only one form of communication and a rather limited one at that. Sometimes we act as though it were the only arrow in our quiver: we pull it out whenever we do not know what else to do. But we could expand our repertoire of effective communication. Working with speech also includes learning to work with silence. Being aware of the power of silence makes it possible to consciously choose when to speak and when not to speak, what to say and what not to say, rather than just blurting out whatever pops into our head.

When we control our speech, it becomes a support for being present rather than an obstacle to it. Mindless talk distances us from our immediate experience and depletes our ability to stay with what is happening. Presence is about staying with the circumstances we are facing and not wiggling out. This does not mean that we just resign ourselves to putting up with whatever comes our way. It does not mean that we do not try to find solutions, treatments, or cures. It simply means that we do so from a point of engagement rather than from a conceptual and experiential distance.

At the emotional level, to be present, we need to learn how to be still with our emotions. As humans, we live in an emotional world, and those emotions have strong effects on us. We can learn to appreciate emotions in all their vividness without dulling them or being overwhelmed by them. A basic guideline for dealing with emotions is neither to indulge our emotions nor to cover them up. Being present does not mean getting rid of emotions in order to stay calm. It is the ability to stay calm within the emotional world we inhabit. Emotions have real value. At the same time, we can avoid falling prey to their traps. Emotions are like storms blowing across a mountain. Even when those storms are roaring, the mountain holds still. Sometimes the mountain benefits as old deposits of dirt are blown away and the air is cleared. Sometimes the mountain suffers as the wind and water beat away at it and begin to break it down. But in either case, the mountain just sits there with presence and dignity.

In the same way that we get caught up in nervous chatter in our speech, we can get seduced by interior mental chatter. This restlessness of mind is the major obstacle to the ability to be present. It is mind run wild. Unless we find a way to rein in this runaway discursiveness, our quality of presence will be limited. To work with this obstacle, the first step is to notice how distracted we are. When we begin to see the full extent of our distractedness, we may feel discouraged. In fact, becoming aware of our distractedness is a key breakthrough. Often we are so distracted that we don't even recognize it. We are so caught up in distraction that we have no way of seeing it. As soon as we recognize our distractedness, we have taken a step back from it. We have an alternative. We awaken the suspicion that distractedness is not our only option. That suspicion is a powerful inspiration to work with our mind, both through formal meditation practice and as we go about our life.

Being present is based on the cultivation of mindfulness in whatever we do. Through mindfulness, we develop greater composure and a heightened sensitivity to nonverbal communication. Then, to the extent that we ourselves are present, we can radiate that same quality outward to the people around us. It is hard to be generous, disciplined, or patient if we are not fully present. If we are present and attentive, and our mind is flexible, we are more receptive to the environment around us. When we are working with the dying, this ability to pick up on the environment is invaluable. The more present we are, the more we can tune in to what is happening. At the same time, that quality of presence is contagious. The dying person picks up on it. The people around him pick up on it. Presence is a powerful force. It settles the environment so that people can begin to relax.

Working with the slogan "Be present" does not mean that we have to plunk ourselves down and practice formal sitting meditation when we are with dying persons. Although that can be a very powerful thing to do, it is not always possible; and for some people, the formality of that approach could be an obstacle. But we can take the same quality of presence cultivated in sitting practice and extend that out. No matter what we encounter, whether it is possible for us to practice formally or not, we can still put ourselves in touch with that sense of simplicity and attentiveness, the basic presence that formal meditation cultivates—and project that out. We are learning to value nonaction, *being* as well as *doing*, and we are communicating that quality to others.

A friend of mine was working with a young man who was close to death from AIDS. As a string of visitors came and went, paying their last respects, the man's breathing became increasingly tense and labored. Later, watching the man struggling to breathe, my friend decided to just sit quietly with him and observe what was going on. There was not that much to do, and rather than trying to occupy himself or figure out ways to keep busy, my friend just sat there breathing in and breathing out— and the more he settled, the more the young man followed, until the dying man's breathing was as smooth and unlabored as my friend's. My friend was able to have a powerful effect on that person, even though on the surface, he had neither said anything nor done anything other than just sit there.

We can work with the sick and dying without ever really being present. It is tempting to remove ourselves mentally, psychically, and emotionally, if not physically. This is especially so at the time when we see clearly that death is on the way and there is "nothing more to be done." Being present with the sick or dying—not checking in and checking out emotionally and mentally, but staying put—is difficult. It is uncomfortably raw and basic and makes demands on our core resources as human beings.

Being present has a quality of stability that can communicate in the midst of activity as well as when we are sitting still. That stability is like an anchor or a lifeline. No matter what is swirling around, no matter how chaotic or difficult the situation, that sense of presence is a stabilizing force. When we fly off or lose contact with what is going on, we can touch back in through that sense of presence. It is completely reliable, like the earth.

For many people, their only contact with serious illness is in the forbidding, alien, and high-tech atmosphere of the hospital or clinic. Hospitals are busy, active, noisy places where the focus is on battling disease. In that battle between the healers and the disease, the actual living people involved often get lost. Working with this slogan to bring even a small element of simple presence into the hubbub of a hospital setting is of great value.

20

Walking through the Door

WHENEVER WE GROUND OUR ACTIONS in awareness and compassion, whatever we do will be helpful and effective. However, our awareness and compassion are not at all steady—they come and go. One moment we are in touch with them, and the next moment they are gone. When we are working with dying people, we see that contrast—between awareness and nonawareness, genuine compassion and distorted compassion—over and over again, and we have an opportunity to work with it.

Each time we walk through the door of a dying person's room, we have a chance to reconnect with our awareness and compassion. We set the tone for our entire encounter in those first few minutes, when we first make contact with the dying person and the people around him. When we enter the room of a dying person, it is vitally important that we enter properly. This means that we must let go of our previous concerns and theories, our strategies and tactics, as we enter. If we drop that baggage at the door, we can take an unstructured look at what is going on instead of relying on our favorite prepackaged approach. Usually, there is more to learn from the situation at hand than from what we bring to it. However, it is not easy to enter nakedly, with no props, for that requires that we tolerate a moment of discomfort and uncertainty, a moment when we have not quite figured the whole thing out. Each time we enter, we are vulnerable and groundless—but in the tenderness of that moment, we are receptive to new insight.

If we enter a person's room mindfully and with sensitivity, we can then provide attentive care—the care that comes from paying attention to the environment first and our theories second. We provide whatever we can, based on what seems to be needed at the time rather than being compelled to blindly fulfill some preestablished mandate. What we provide could be offering a sip of water, engaging in a conversation, giving an injection, or opening the drapes—or it could be just sitting with a dying person and not doing very much at all. Attentive care is responding to what comes up rather than clinging to results or hoping for a cure.

When I was with my father just before his death, I observed how various nurses entered his hospital room. At times, it was painful for me to watch. As it became obvious to everyone that my father was dying, some nurses continued to relate with him just as before, in a very ordinary and personable fashion. They were at ease with his death and could talk to him in a relaxed way—but other nurses abruptly changed their pattern of relationship. They would dash into the room, check the chart or do some procedure, and dash back out—literally not once looking to the right or the left. They hid behind their routines to avoid dealing with him. The most extreme case was a nurse who barged into the room, bustled over to the bed, and cheerily declared, "It's time for your vitamins." I looked at her and said, "You've got to be kidding! Vitamins?" It was so far beside the point that it was humorous. There was not the slightest flexibility in this nurse's routine, for if she had paused even for an instant, she would have seen how irrelevant it was to administer vitamins to someone only hours away from death. Attentive care is possible only if we take the time to stop and look.

In attentive care, our basic intention is to enter the sick person's world. Instead of bringing in our world and imposing it on her, we are accepting that person's world as it is—her confusion, pain, fear, sense of injustice, whatever she is experiencing. When we do so, we may be shocked to discover that her view of the world is very different from ours. We may totally disagree with the way in which she is responding to her death. On top of that, there may be tremendous confusion and emotional disturbance among the people surrounding the dying person—her family, the hospital staff, or whoever else is present. But we could *still* step into that world. We could walk through the door and enter that swirling, confusing atmosphere rather than standing back and protecting ourselves.

In working with someone who is dying, there is a tremendous temptation to ignore our own relationship to death and immediately assume the role of the helper. But when we do so, we are losing our common ground with that person. Entering a dying person's world takes courage and empathy. Only by accepting our own vulnerability to death do we overcome the divided perspective of "I (over here) am helping you (over there)." Only then are we in the same boat. So in a sense, we need to be willing to die *with* that person. Usually we do not want to be in the same boat at all. Although it is embarrassing to admit, we are secretly glad that it is *someone else* who has cancer and *we* are the one looking after him rather than the other way around. We find security in the fact that we are not the one who is sick right now. It is hard not to feel that way, even when we are sincerely and earnestly trying to help.

There is no point in hiding that tendency and pretending to have empathy. Instead of feigning benevolence, we could acknowledge that we are afraid of sickness, afraid that the same thing might happen to us, and we are desperate to distance ourselves from that possibility. We could look into that fear and see how it operates. Beginning at the beginning, we could notice how we enter a sick person's room. What concerns come up in our mind? How do we view that person? How much can we identify with her situation? When do we shut down? Where are we holding back? What are our limits? Being honest about our limitations protects us from becoming patronizing and self-satisfied. When we are more honest, we don't have as much to prove. We accept who we are and go from there. So our whole approach lightens. At the same time, we also relieve the people with whom we are dealing from having to prove themselves to us. So there are fewer barriers; we are less separate. When we approach a sick or dying person, we are simply relating to her as an ordinary human being, in the same category as ourselves.

Working with others gives us constant feedback as to our own state of mind. Spending time with dying people is revealing. It reflects back to us with great honesty and vividness our own current relationship with uncertainty, death, and imperma-nence. It exposes our shortcomings and cuts through our pre-tenses. If we are open to this feedback, we can sharpen our understanding of who we are and reawaken our humor. We are reminded over and over again not to take ourselves so seriously. Although we may dream that we are going to be the one who steps in and, just in the nick of time, helps some dying person realize his or her human potential, I doubt whether any of us is going to accomplish that very often. If we have some humor about ourselves, we realize that we, too, are involved in a slow process of growth. We are working with our own states of mind, just as other people are working with theirs. We are also dying, just as they are. We are all in this together.

21

How to Help

ONCE WE HAVE ENTERED, after we have walked through the door, we can change the environment for the better by the way in which we connect with people. If we are as simple and non-judgmental as possible, and if we work with our own state of mind, we can make a genuine connection with the dying person and the people around him.

Trungpa Rinpoche used the phrase *one death* as a guide for working with people who are dying. That does not mean jumping into the pyre so we burn up together, like widowed brides in India. Instead, it means that the way we can connect with the person who is dying is through our shared experience of loss and death. Prior to the experience of physical death, our life is filled with many little deaths, disruptions and losses both large and small. The key is to acknowledge those gaps in our experience. If we are aware of the discontinuity in our own lives, we can connect with people who are facing that same discontinuity in a heightened way at the time of death. The ground where we meet one another is unstructured.

You might think you have nothing to offer. You just enter the dying person's room and feel helpless. Even if you are a doctor or nurse, you cannot necessarily save a person. It's true. We may not be able to prevent someone from dying or being in pain. Chances are, we have no magical pill to stop either the pain or the suffering that goes with it, so it can be very frustrating. We may wonder, "What *do* I have to offer? What *do* I have to give?" — especially if we are not a medical professional, a healer, a priest, or some high Tibetan lama. But in fact, there are many ways we can be of help. Even if there seems to be very little we can do, we can still help people by our presence of mind and by what we project out. We *can* affect the environment for the better.

NOT HANDING OUT ADVICE

We could begin by accepting people as they are rather than trying to change them. It is quite common for people who are sick or dying to be bombarded with all sorts of advice. They are magnets for it. People who would not ordinarily go around telling their friends how to conduct their lives suddenly transform into pundits and experts once their friends fall ill. We are so anxious to help that we don't wait to be asked; we just launch in. And we have all sorts of opinions and criticisms as to how our friends are doing and how they should be handling their situation. It is easier to hide out in those opinions and become judgmental and demanding than to let go of our expectations and ideas and be left with nothing to hang on to. But that nothing-to-hang-on-to point is where we can actually make a connection.

It is not easy to resist this urge to fix things and make them go our way. However, all those demands place a terrible burden on others. They are based on rejection, not acceptance, and they create barriers that separate us from one another. We could work to reverse that pattern by accepting the sick or dying person as she is without trying to make her please us by how she goes about things. That might not sound like much, but it is rare. Especially when someone is sick or in a weakened state, it is common for people to pile in and lay heavy trips on her: "You should die this way," "You should die that way," "You should relate to your state of mind this way," "You should relate to your state of mind that way." So merely to have someone visit who doesn't immediately start with "You should do this, and you should do that; you should feel this, and you should feel that" is a gift. It is unusual to encounter someone who doesn't immediately hand out advice.

SEEING THE ORDINARINESS OF DEATH

Beyond that, we can help by not taking the view that death is a big mistake. Daniel Callahan, the medical ethicist, once said, "Despite the casual talk in our culture of death as 'a part of life,' I believe that, in reality, the dominant view is actually that of death as an outsider." In our culture, unfortunately, death is often seen as a mistake, a failure, a breakdown. Something has gone terribly wrong, and everybody feels it. The person dying feels that she has made some big mistake and is *disappointing* everybody by dying—and the people around her feel angry, as though she had failed them in some way by forcing them to have to deal with this messy and painful situation. There is no recognition of the ordinariness of death, no acceptance of the fact that it happens to everyone.

Death is natural to life. It is not a mistake, sad though it may be. When we encounter death in our lives, for whatever reason, death just happens to be what is going on. It does not help to make a dying person feel guilty that he is dying or that he is doing something wrong. He should not need to apologize to us for dying or try to hide it from us because it is too embarrassing. It is more helpful to respect death as it is—a powerful and challenging experience that is at the same time quite ordinary and to be expected.

EXPRESSING FRIENDSHIP IN THE
FACE OF DEATH

Expressing our friendship is the most simple and powerful way we can help. This may be difficult because, when we know we are losing someone, there may be a tendency to close off. Expressing friendship in the face of death takes incredible gallantry. It means that we are willing to express our love, even though the *person* we love will not last, *we* will not last, and *the relationship* between the two of us will not last. Whether the person we love is around for a minute or a decade, we are willing to love him nonetheless. If a dying person is lucky enough to encounter friendship like that, he will not be held back by that friendship but supported. Instead of feeling mired in our neediness as if in glue, he will feel freed by our affection.

Of course, we may not feel gallant at all; we may feel needy, because we do not want to lose that person—or *anyone* we care about, for that matter. In an intense situation such as illness or death, every tiny shift of mind is magnified. The encounter with death is likely to be emotionally powerful and, at times, overwhelming. We are apt to be caught up in all sorts of conflicting emotions. We want to do what is right for the person, but at the same time, we are filled with resentment, grasping, and confusion. We want to be loving and supportive, but at the same time, we do not want to deal with that person at all. It is just too painful to handle.

In the midst of that kind of intensity, it is not easy to deal with our mind as we bounce from one emotional extreme to another. When we see that happening, we need to take a break, regroup, and make a fresh start. We could acknowledge that confusion, accept it, and then let it go. Confusion arises out of our own fear and grasping. As we become more familiar with our own mental extremes, such as through the practice of sitting meditation, we are less likely to be thrown by the intensity of our own thoughts. We have seen such intense and fearful thoughts and emotions come and go over and over again. We have become familiar with our thought process and seen how it affects us. We recognize our own emotional patterns. So when we are overwhelmed in the face of death, and the intensity of our emotions and thoughts begins to build, we recognize what is going on. That familiarity is what enables us to let go of those thoughts and resettle ourselves. We can bring ourselves back to earth.

COMMUNICATING HONESTLY

In an environment of fear, honesty is in short supply. Dying people are frequently and routinely lied to. Often this is done with the best of intentions, such as that we want to cheer them up, we want to make them feel better, we want them not to lose hope. But the result is that dying people notice that they are being monitored. They feel compelled to be careful about what they say so as not to upset the people around them or rock the boat. The atmosphere around dying people is permeated with subtle expectations. There may be a group conspiracy to uphold the pretense that everything is going to be OK, in which everybody in the room knows what is going on, but no one will talk about it. There is this *Big Unspoken Fact* that nobody is willing to deal with. Everybody is busy dancing around the reality of the situation, and each person is trying to protect everyone else all the time to the point of absurdity. But ultimately, no one is protected. Instead, everyone is uptight and afraid he might slip up and say the wrong thing—including, of course, the person who is dying.

It is important to tell dying people the truth. When possible, we should always let a dying person know that she is dying. Often that is not news to her. We are merely confirming what she already knows. Hiding the truth only makes the whole situation more painful. Most people can tell when they are being lied to, even if they don't let on. When we lie, it undermines the dying person's trust, and she no longer knows whom or what to believe. Not only that, but we have taken away her opportunity to absorb what is going on and prepare herself to die.

Communicating skillfully about something as basic and profound as life and death is not easy. There is a lot of fear involved in talking about death. If someone has been battling a prolonged illness, people around him may think that if he hears the bad news, he will give up. So they conspire to keep up his hope and thereby keep him alive a little longer. A friend of mind encountered such a conspiracy of hope when he brought up the issue of talking with his father about death. His brother screamed at him, as though he were being disloyal to even think of raising the issue with his father. His father's doctor and the medical staff went along with his brother's wishes and did not talk frankly with the father. Throughout his father's terminal illness, everyone in the hospital consistently treated the man as though everything were going to be fine. This deceptive approach was painful for my friend, and he suspected that it was painful for his father as well—but the wall of silence was impenetrable. Everyone was constantly watching everyone else, making sure each person was doing his part to uphold the conspiracy.

It is not easy to know how to talk with someone who is dying, and often, physical barriers to communication seem overwhelming. A person may be in a coma, hallucinating, or unable to hear. As with all communication, without sensitivity and proper timing, nothing you say will be heard. People sometimes take the guideline of telling the truth to dying people as if it were graven in stone, so they march in proclaiming, "It's important that you recognize right now the fact that you are dying. You're not relating to this! You're watching television! Snap out of it!" Just blurting out something like that is not in the least helpful, but people do crazy things like that.

Communication doesn't work when it comes out of the blue; we must first establish some kind of connection. We can communicate more easily if we understand and accept the various states of mind sick and dying people experience. Those states of mind are apt to be intense, rapidly changing, and not at all what we might hope. There tends to be a lot of messiness around pain and illness. Some people withdraw into themselves; some lose their rationality, seeing visions and hallucinating; others drift in and out of consciousness. People's mental and emotional states may be altered due to their age, the nature of their illnesses, and their medications. It therefore makes sense to learn something about their symptoms and what they are dealing with physically, so that we can figure out a way to reach them.

TALKING SIMPLY

It is hard to know how much a sick person is perceiving. According to Tibetan Buddhist teachings, in the transition from life to death, people are a lot more aware than they might appear to be. In that case, our operating assumption should be that they *do* understand, even though they may not respond in their usual way. People who are very close to death may seem totally unresponsive, but even if someone is just lying there immobile, he may very well be able to hear what we are saying. So we could still say simple things like "I love you" or "I will miss you." In addition, it is said that a person's intuitive perception at the point of death is greatly heightened, so nonverbal communication is picked up on extremely easily and quickly. That means that our state of mind and the energy we put out communicate very powerfully at that time—for better or for worse. Given that fact, it is important to try to affect things for the better.

If our communication is too complicated, we will not connect. We need to simplify. If we pay attention to how we speak, and how we express ourselves generally, we can learn to get across what we have to say in a few well-chosen words or gestures. Often people are far too complicated. A person who is dealing with illness and physical pain isn't usually up for long philosophical discussions on the nature of reality. It might be much more communicative to apply a nice, cool washcloth to his forehead or to say a word or two and then be quiet. Just sitting with someone can be the best thing.

When we are nervous and a little uncomfortable, we tend to fall back on what is easy and familiar. This can result in a kind of chatty approach in which we try to engage the dying person verbally in order to avoid the discomfort of silence. That might make *us* feel better for a little while, but it doesn't help the dying person very much. Not a lot of real communication is happening; instead, one person is lying there, and this other person is yapping and yapping. We do not want to create a situation in which the dying person needs to humor *us*! That is putting the whole thing backward: we are saddling her with the burden of trying to make *us* feel OK that *she* is dying! Sadly, that happens all the time. There is an old maxim that goes, "At the very least, don't make a nuisance of yourself." This certainly applies here. In fact, there is an entire book, *How to Be a Help and Not a Nuisance*, that elaborates on that saying and how it can be applied. If you cannot be helpful, at least don't be a nuisance. A humble guideline, but fundamental.

NOT FREAKING OUT

Through our behavior and how we manifest, we can either help a person or add to his pain and confusion. The environment we create around the dying person affects him deeply. If the environment becomes too hectic, chaotic, and emotionally charged, it can be a real hindrance; and if it is gentle, open, and accepting, it can be a real support. So although it is good to be able to express our natural feelings of grief and sorrow, it is not helpful to act out all over the place because we happen to be freaked out. If we are really losing it, it is better to leave the room for a while than to stay. We can be gentle to ourselves and give ourselves a place to rant and rave, to sob and cry, to express our grief and pain in any way that suits us. Afterward, when we are more settled, we can return to the dying person's room. It is a delicate choice, when to stay and when to leave, and we can help one another with this decision. By knowing when to step out of the room, we can dig into our feelings and express them — and at the same time promote a sane and accommodating atmosphere around the dying person.

DEALING WITH PAIN AND SUFFERING

One of the most difficult things about tending to the sick and dying is the amount of pain and suffering that is involved. There are many different kinds of pain, and every illness has different characteristic patterns. Some illnesses are excruciatingly painful, whereas others cause only minor pain. At any level, pain can often be treated or moderated by medication, and there is absolutely no reason not to do that unless the dying person himself prefers otherwise. Yet the management of pain is not a simple matter, and both undertreatment and overtreatment are common. Most difficult of all, there are occasionally people who suffer pain so severe that no treatment seems able to alleviate it.

On top of that, both the people treating the pain and the people being treated have all sorts of ideas about pain. For instance, patients who are terminally ill may nonetheless still fear the stigma of addiction. People can be very puritanical, thinking that when someone is dying, she shouldn't have any drugs at all, that she should just deal with everything straight. We may worry

that painkilling drugs will dull awareness and advise whoever is
dying to do without them. It is easy for us to give advice, since
we ourselves are not in pain, but in fact, being in excruciating
pain *itself* dulls awareness. Pain makes it hard for a person to
clarify her thoughts and know what is going on. Furthermore,
even if a dying person does not use any painkilling drugs, she
may still be confused. So there's nothing wrong with relieving
pain. And fortunately, now there are many drugs available that
can relieve pain while at the same time reducing mental confusion rather than contributing to it. But pain is only one part of
the picture — the other is suffering.

Pain and suffering are not the same thing. By understanding
the difference between the two, you can be more clear about
where you can help and where you cannot. You may be able to
reduce someone's pain with medication, but you are unlikely to
find a pill for suffering. Suffering can occur for all sorts of reasons
that have nothing to do with physical pain. A person may be
suffering because he is afraid to die or because he is worried
about what is going to happen to his family. A person may be
suffering because his family is feuding or because of the humilia-
tion of having to be taken care of by other people. He may be
suffering because he yearns for the return of physical vigor and
health, because he feels ugly and disfigured by disease, because
his mind isn't as clear as he would like, or because he is just not
the person he used to be. He may be suffering from all sorts of
regrets and disappointments about his life, from a sense of lost
opportunities, or because of money worries. Suffering has countless causes.

In working with a person, we will not be able to alleviate
her suffering unless we understand its source. Figuring out the
cause of someone's suffering can be a slow and difficult process,
but if we do not make the effort to do so, it will be easy to assume
one thing when in fact something entirely different is going on.
Some people are not that bothered by circumstances that for

other people would be a hellish experience. For instance, being weak and needing to be taken care of would be a very big deal indeed for some people, but it might not be that big a deal for other people. For those people, however, something *else* might be a very big deal, like not being able to drink alcohol. We may have no clue what is causing someone to be upset. As we try this and that to relieve the dying person's suffering, we find that we are mainly aware of what would bother *us*. What is really bothering another person could be something totally different from what we expected or what seems most obvious to us. It could be something that seems bizarre or insignificant, like a misplaced watch or the color of the wall.

A student of mine was working in home care, taking care of an elderly man who lived alone in his house. His client was in reasonably good health, and things were going along fine. But just as the man's pain started to get under control, he began to go downhill. As his pain decreased, his suffering seemed to intensify. His decline began in December, when he started to fall down frequently. My student would find him fallen in the bathroom or here or there around the house, but there was no obvious reason for it. It took my student a long time to figure out what was really going on. It turned out that his client's wife had died the previous year right around that same time; furthermore, they were approaching her birthday, which fell during the holidays. This was going to be the man's first holiday without her, and he was quietly trying to kill his pain, and perhaps himself as well, by taking extra doses of his medications. He didn't need these medications from a pain standpoint; it was his suffering he was trying to cure. And for that, his painkillers were ineffective. When my student realized what that client was trying to do, he was able to intervene and help the man to acknowledge the emotional suffering he was going through. He could help the man accept the loss he had experienced and go on living.

ALLOWING CHAOS

Developing a sane approach to death and dying depends on being willing to work with a lot of rough edges, both our own and others'. Dying people may be freaked out and unable to deal with their situation at all, raging and fighting and upset. A person who seems to be doing OK one day may the next day suddenly take a turn for the worse—and just when we get used to *that*, then all at once he takes a turn for the better again. When that happens, we are less and less certain *what* is really going on, and we begin to lose track of where we stand. We flip-flop continually and find our mind drifting from day to day, or even minute to minute, wondering what is happening. Is he about to die, or is he going to live? Is it a miraculous recovery or a mental trick? Does he have a long time or no time at all? Our mind does somersaults.

In the midst of that confusion, the focus to come back to is that of being just two simple human beings present together on the shared ground of uncertainty. On that ground, there is room for all sorts of chaos. In our society, we like to manage everything and make it neat and clean and nice. It is tempting to try to micromanage death as well, because we don't want to deal with our own emotional extremes; nor do we particularly want to deal with the physical messiness of death. In other words, we don't want to deal with a real person dying. So everyone has to be clean and orderly and polite. The dying person, thank you very much, should keep a stiff upper lip in order to die a good death and not bother us by freaking out. "Let's all be really nice, and that will be great. Let's all play nice music, and nobody will have to deal with anything raw."

That attempt to smooth death over may be tempting, but it is a trap. The semireligious atmosphere we create becomes a gooey, cloying cocoon. Everything seems peaceful and sweet, but only superficially. If we put pink frosting on a cake full of worms, it may look very pretty, but eventually the worms will start to surface. So creating a peaceful atmosphere artificially by glossing over our fears and suppressing anything unpleasant does not work. That is not truly peaceful; it is avoiding reality. An atmosphere that includes what is raw along with what is beautiful and tender is more disturbing, but it is also more honest. Ultimately, it is more peaceful as well—because there is less that can threaten it, since a certain amount of chaos and disorder is expected and accepted. That kind of peace is palpable and real and not at all artificial.

DEALING WITH THE POLITICS OF DYING

In dealing with death, politics is rampant. It is very rare to be working simply with one other person, one-on-one. Usually there's a whole collection of people. In addition to medical personnel, there are relatives and friends and people from different backgrounds and understandings who may not agree on *anything*—whether to stay in the hospital or go home, whether to tell the truth or not, whether to do this ceremony or that. In dealing with all that, it is important to be clearheaded and politically savvy.

The medical establishment has all sorts of rules and regulations, conventions, and group neuroses around the subject of death, and health-care workers may be operating on automatic pilot. So whenever someone is hospitalized, we need to pay attention to what is happening if we want to look out for the dying person's interests. A dying person may not be able to speak up for herself or have any clout. In that case, practically speaking, she needs a spokesperson who is willing to ask questions: "Wait a minute, why are you doing this procedure? She does not want that done." In a hospital, even a very good one, it is always advisable to have a friend who is able and willing to deal with the authorities. Otherwise, we will be swept along by the prevailing ethic, whether we agree with it or not. We need to have someone whom we trust to decide when to speak up and when to let things run their course.

Even when we are in a position to help in that way, we do not always have all the options we might like, so we must be quick on our feet and do what we can, knowing that we will not always get our way. Even though we may feel strongly that our friend wants to go home, her spouse or relatives may say, "No way, we're going to try everything possible to prolong her life" — and we may lack the authority to do anything about it. So we have to be able to deal with the fact that things may not work out as we would like, and even though we may have a lot of ideas about what would be best, we may not be able to carry out those ideas. That is sad but true.

MAINTAINING A SENSE OF HUMOR

People don't usually associate humor with death. Death is supposed to be solemn, just like religion. But humor can be liberating in the face of sickness and death. By humor, I do not mean cracking jokes, although jokes definitely have their place; I mean not taking ourselves too seriously.

We all die: death is a human experience; it is not all that unique. But it is hard to be natural in the presence of death or include it in our lives as we do other experiences. We tend to relegate it to a special category with prescribed roles to play. With that approach, nobody acts like a real human anymore. Instead, those involved are like actors in an imaginary hospital and deathbed scene.

I had a friend who was dying of breast cancer that had spread throughout her body. Over the course of her last year, she had many close calls. People would gather around to pay their final respects, but she would always bounce back. What I noticed is that when I went to see her, I would put on what I assumed to be a proper demeanor for paying final respects. I am not sure how I cooked up the idea of what that demeanor should be—maybe from the movies. Since my friend kept not dying, I was eventually able to see what I was doing. The mask I was putting on was completely phony. I had no humor.

Thanks to the erratic course of my friend's illness, by the time she did die, I was able to walk into her room with my humor and humanity intact. I had seen through the contrivances of my imagined proper deathbed scene, and at that point, a glimmer of humor broke through. Something lifted. I was able to be more present and also more ordinary, more raw in the presence of death. I have always considered that insight a great gift my dying friend gave me.

When we lose our humor, our whole demeanor changes—our tone of voice, how we move and carry ourselves, our facial expressions. This may sound strange, but it happens. We may be trying to help, but when we approach sick or dying people in that way, they do not feel better; they feel weird. They pick up on the fact that the people around them are acting strangely, walking on eggshells, oddly quiet, trying not to disturb or upset anyone. It is sad, because without humor, there is no room for ordinary interaction. Everything is "heavy." We can't have a normal conversation with someone anymore because all we can focus on is his death. "Forget about wanting to know whether Cleveland or New York won; you should be beyond all that now." We want no frivolity; we want *profound* communication only. But that is not all that helpful—in fact, it is insulting.

It does not matter whether a person is gravely sick or the victim of some dreadful trauma or how close to death he is—he is still alive. He doesn't want to be suddenly cut off from regular life and see everyone around him act like visitors to a funeral home.

Sick and dying people do not exist on a separate plane from the rest of us. I think we try to put them in a special category because it distances us from the experience of sickness and death. It is a way of protecting ourselves by focusing on how different they are from us rather than on how similar we are. In contrast, humor maintains a sense of ordinary life and simple human contact.

OUR UNDERSTANDING, behavior, attitudes, and emotions all have an effect on the environment around us. Handing out advice, letting our mind run wild, creating an atmosphere of lies and deception, giving up on communication, being too complicated, chattering nervously, confusing pain and suffering, freaking out, micromanaging, smoothing things over, giving in to politics and bureaucracy, maintaining an atmosphere of heavy-handed solemnity, denying the ordinariness of death—these are just a few of the many ways we affect the environment for the worse. But it is also possible to affect the environment for the better. We could look into the harmful patterns to which we fall prey and cultivate our ability to be simpler, less judgmental, and more aware of our mental and emotional state moment to moment. Then, as these obstacles arise, we might recognize them and be able to let them go.

22

Letting Go

EACH PART OF THIS BOOK deals with a different form of letting go. Part One is about letting go of ignorance, preconceptions, and fear. Part Two is about letting go of self-absorption and ego-centeredness. Part Three is about letting go of the many barriers that arise as we attempt to help one another. It is about dropping our reliance on prepackaged strategies and being willing to work spontaneously and courageously with whatever arises. Letting go is not something that we do once and then are done with it. It is an ongoing process. In that process, each time we let go even a little, we create an opening for something unexpected to take place. Each time we let go, we see our world more freshly.

When we walk into the room of someone who is sick or dying, we do not know what we will find there. If we think we know already, before we look, we are mistaken. If we have convinced ourselves about what is going to be there ahead of time, we will no longer be able to see what's *really* going on. In order to see clearly, we need to go back to the point of total ignorance—the point at which we know nothing. Even if we were in the room the day before, it may be very different when we go back. The dying person could be in a totally different state—and we may be different as well. But we will miss that if we don't momentarily reconnect, even for the briefest instant, with that unknowing mind. It may be just a slight pause, just a reminder—

but it lets us *first* see what is happening and *then* do something. Over and over, we prepare ourselves and let go. It is important to take the time to study and develop the skills we need to be able to help others. At the same time, we must let go of all that and rest simply for an undefined moment in unstructured experience. Each time we walk through the door, we need to start anew.

When I was in the middle of my class on *The Tibetan Book of the Dead* at the Naropa Institute, just before one of my classes, Trungpa Rinpoche called me into a lengthy meeting. During the course of the meeting, I was getting more and more uptight. I was not at all ready for the upcoming class. Rinpoche had offered to help me when I agreed to teach the class in the first place, so I asked him what he thought I should do. I had my empty note cards ready and was hoping for an outline or some topical suggestions—but instead Rinpoche told me to walk into the classroom, take my seat, look at the white wall—and *wait*. He told me that if I did that, something definitely would come up. When I asked more generally about teaching, his advice was to take the time to prepare but, at the start of each class, drop that preparation completely and begin afresh. Although I can still remember that pause before my Naropa class, a pause that seemed to last about a year, at the same time, I remember that amazingly I did figure out something to say that day.

In facing new experience or in facing death, eventually we need to let go of our supports and trust what happens. We need to free ourselves from relying on any props whatsoever. That does not mean we need not prepare ourselves intellectually and emotionally or train our mind and heart through meditation and contemplative practices such as tonglen. Those things are important—but at some point, after all that hard work, we need to drop everything and take a leap. Each time we take such a leap, it is tremendously liberating. We discover that death is teaching us how to be completely alive.

INDEX